FINDING MY FATHER

"Shannon Reynolds hits a home run in *Finding My Father*, exposing her own harrowing journey with raw transparency and meaningful authenticity. With short chapters, amazing readability, and riveting real-life drama, she points the reader to the only solution for those searching for a father's love and attention. Many today are experiencing the emotional pain of fatherlessness, whether the father was abusive, careless, or simply not there. I must say I had a difficult time putting this book down once I began reading it. "

- Dr. Dave Williams/ Dave Williams Ministries

FINDING MY FATHER

By Shannon Reynolds

(As told to A.K. Hartline)

Printed in the United States of America

First Printing, 2018

For more information, contact:

Shannon Reynolds
P.O. Box 324
Howard, OH 43028

5

For Woodrow Parker Sr. who loved unconditionally, and for my stepfather, Gordon Howard, who was a perfect example of an earthly father, I love you both, and I'll see you both in Heaven someday!

FOREWORD

By Mr. Nicky Cruz

Loser. Idiot. You deserve it!

This is what someone might naturally feel when reading Shannon's story. "How can someone suffer this much abuse, betrayal, and rejection and it not be their fault?", you might wonder.

But a lot of us come from a world like this that is not normal. Not fair. Full of pain and hardship. Seeing too much hell and brokenness at a young age. Like I did. A world that is all too common.

I see Shannon's story much differently. Because I have been through much of what she has, and have seen and survived the other side of life. The side few want to recognize or talk about.

Fearless. Unflinching. Brave.

This is what I feel as Shannon bravely tells her story. Refusing to sugar coat a life that was destined to end up in tragedy - a mere statistic soon to be forgotten - in a world that seems to be without hope. Yet, hoping beyond hope, something (Someone) kept driving her to survive, to not give up.

Relentless.

Whereas at one time only the elusive high would drive Shannon to get up from each beat down, from each set back, from each arrest, now she is driven by a different call.

<u>This story has to be heard and told again and again</u>. It is not a story that is just from the ghetto, or the lower class, or the less fortunate. It is affecting us all. Drugs, rejection, fatherlessness, abuse - they are all equal opportunity killers.

But there is an antidote, an answer, a hope, a way out. And Shannon land Scott are fearlessly and passionately telling

The Story. And you will find that answer proclaimed loudly in *Finding My Father*!

Nicky Cruz

Evangelist and author of 17 books, including the international bestseller *Run Baby Run.*

Summer, 1998:

The police officers who worked that beat knew me well, and one evening, just after I had purchased two crack rocks, a cop car pulled up alongside me as I sashayed coolly along.

"Hey, where're you going Fruit Lucy?" he hollered. I recognized him - he was a skinny one who had arrested me a couple of times before.

"Just going to the store!"

"Come on, I know what you're doing!"

He braked and got out, and I quickly popped the two rocks into my mouth.

"You holding anything, girl?" he asked. "Up against the car, you know the drill."

I did. It wasn't my first rodeo. I spread, hands on the roof, and he frisked me, finding my crack pipe and a single rock in my pocket. I had totally forgotten about that one.

"Okay, this is enough to take you in Lucy. Never going to learn, are you?"

I had to get rid of the rocks in my mouth. I saw my chance as he opened the door, and I spit them in the grass on the other side of the walkway.

He cuffed me, not very tightly I noticed, and put me in the back of the cruiser.

"Let's take a ride downtown," he said.

"Okay," I responded, as though I had a choice in the matter. But my mind was working feverishly on a plan of escape. I had to get to those rocks; if I didn't, and soon, someone else would find them and take them and I couldn't have that, couldn't dare let that happen.

I was in the grip of paranoia and obsession at that stage in my life, the crack pipe and drugs all consuming, altering my perception of reality. There was a time, not that long ago it seemed, when I would awake to the day and be okay for a bit before I smoked, but not now. Now, I had a rock at the ready, and almost as soon as I opened my eyes I lit up and stayed high until my head hit the pillow at night, if I even went to sleep.

"… gotta try sometime", the officer said, something I didn't catch.

These handcuffs are loose enough, I bet I can slide right out of them, I thought. *And if I can do that, I can slide that metal door open between the front and back, get up there and kick this skinny copper in the head!* I could do it too. I had gotten tough over the years, in and out of jail, living on the streets. I had once been a weak sister, afraid to fight, bullied by those girls in high school, but boy they wouldn't want to face me now!

Anyway, if I could get to him, I could distract him enough to get him to pull over and I could escape out the front passenger side door. Had my plan; now to execute.

It went perfectly.

He pulled off onto the shoulder, braking and tires screeching as I bit his arm and nose and pummeled him about the face.

"Ow!" he screamed, a bit girly, and I would've said something about that but I was busy opening the passenger door and sprinting across the median.

It was cool that my plan had actually worked, but I was one worn out girl by then. A year and a half of heavy drug use, extreme most recently, and malnutrition, had left me emaciated and weak. I was good for the fight to escape, but the fleeing part was not in me. My legs simply gave out and I collapsed, falling to the ground.

It seemed I had only been down for a second, but I was suddenly surrounded by policemen who had answered the officer's call for back up. I tried to get up and run again, but they tackled and hog tied me, feet and hands cuffed together, and I screamed like a madwoman as they carried me to the side of the road. I was dehydrated and delirious, and things were fuzzy around the edges, going in and out of my field of vision.

"I need to go the hospital," I muttered, and they concurred, calling an ambulance to take me.

PART I

The Path Ahead

CHAPTER 1

1973:

I cringed in the closet, curled in the corner, clutching my doll to my chest, something I could console and draw comfort from in these terrifying moments. I could not help my mother. She was, as she had been many times before dating back to my earliest memories, on the receiving end of my drunken father's abuse, both verbal and physical.

I was five years old, and our family lived in a rundown mobile home in a trailer park. My father was a big man, whose chief talents were drinking away whatever money he could make while sober and beating my mother. I would always hide in the closet when he started up, wait until it was over, and then run to the phone and dial the operator. I did this before checking on my mother. I knew the story there anyway: black eyes, bruised pride. The police would haul him off to jail to dry out, and then he would come home. After a brief time out, the vicious cycle would start up again - wash, rinse, repeat.

On one occasion, my mother came running out of the bedroom, on her heels, my drunken father, clad only in his underwear. One of my mother's eyes was swollen shut, and she grabbed the keys to the car off the coffee table and me by the arm, dragging me out the door as my father gave chase, bellowing and wheeling and crashing into things. My mother managed to get us into the car and lock the doors to the old Nova before my father slammed against it, trying the door handle.

"Open this door!" he screamed.

Mom ignored him and started the engine, and he promptly leapt on the hood as she peeled off. I saw his grimacing, growling face as he banged on the windshield, and he swung his big fist hard enough to crack the glass. My mom's response? She gunned the engine and jerked the steering wheel back and forth, throwing him off the car. I saw him slide off and disappear, and my mother drove fast to some friend's house, where we stayed for a couple of days.

But she went back.

Those are the memories I have of my father during those crucial, formative years. He seemed incapable of showing affection to, or spending quality time with, his daughter, and those foundational moments filled with care were entirely absent. I never saw anything redeeming in his spirit. I did not trust him; how could I? He would promise not to drink and beat my mother, and then promptly drink and beat my mother again. I was simply afraid of him. Fear was the only emotion he engendered in my heart.

I was denied the example of a man my father should have provided, paving the way for my emotional stability and healthy relationships throughout life.

But that didn't stop me from searching for him, in all the wrong places for so many wrong years.

CHAPTER 2

By the time I was six years old we had moved into a subdivision in our small town in Tennessee, next door to my grandfather, and soon after I saw a blonde headed girl waving at me from a yard behind his house. I went over to her.

"My name's Kristi," she offered.

"My name's Shannon," I replied.

"Can you come play?"

I asked my mother, she approved, and off we went on a lifetime journey as best friends.

Kristi and I shared so many good times together as children. We rode bikes in the neighborhood, played with Barbie dolls, and I spent almost as much time at her house as my own. She and her parents, Billie Sue and Johnnie, were a major part of my childhood, and Kristi has been a great and loyal friend to me over the years, through the good and the bad. I love her so much to this very day.

My grandfather, Woodrow Parker Sr. was a wonderful, Christian man, kindhearted and the polar opposite of the son he sired. He was selfless and gentle, and he patiently taught me many things, including how to mow grass and cook. I marveled at how different he was from his son, and of course, sought to replace my father with him.

He was also the place my mother and I ran to for rescue from my father when he went on his drunken tirades and attacked us. Eventually, my father straightened up, quit drinking for a while and got a good job in insurance. He would go out of town for extended periods of time on business trips, and when he came home, he would give me gifts: dolls, clothes etc. This was his way of showing that he cared for me, but by then it was too late. If he had done more to build trust and security in me early on, the gifts would mean something. As it was, without true love to back them up, they were hollow and pointless.

My mother somehow endured my father's abuse over the years, emerged with her spirit intact and became a cosmetologist, opening her own salon. When my father came home from his business trips, I heard the arguments, my mother accusing him of infidelity and my father's protests to the contrary. Of course, she was right, and my mother, tired of the years of maltreatment, finally divorced my father. Soon after, she met a wonderful man, Gordon Howard, and they married. He brought with him three beautiful daughters. From the beginning, Gordon tried to be a father to me, but I was jealous of his daughters. They were older, better looking, and they had a father that actually loved them!

I was just eleven years old in the spring of that year, and I was still searching for something to fill the void my father had left in my heart, to numb and take away the cruel pain of the unwanted.

CHAPTER 3

Mr. Holland, an older man who lived next door to my grandfather, was a widower, having lost his wife the prior year. Later into spring I noticed his grass needed cut, and having learned how to mow from my grandfather, I thought I could make a little extra money. My grandfather agreed to let me use his mower for my fledgling business, and I knocked on Mr. Holland's door one sunny day.

"If you need someone to mow your grass, I'd do it for five dollars," I proposed.

He nodded his head and smiled. "Sounds like a reasonable business proposition to me, young lady! Sure, you know how?"

"Oh yes, my grandfather taught me!"

"Well, I'm sure you know what you're doing then! Go to it! If you need anything, let me know!"

After mowing for a while, I needed to use the restroom. Mr. Holland was sitting on the porch, watching me work, and he stood as I approached.

"Can I use your restroom?" I asked, squirming. I had almost held it too long.

"Sure! Right this way," he replied, opening the door. I went and did my business, and when I came out, he was offering me a drink.

"I bet you're thirsty! Here ya go!" he said, pushing the beverage toward me.

"Thanks!" I replied, taking the glass. The liquid was red in color. *Kool - Aid*, I thought, fruity punch and I loved the stuff! I took a drink and my face screwed up. It was strong tasting, definitely not *pure* Kool- Aid, whatever it was!

Mr. Holland watched my expression and chuckled.

"What is this stuff?" I asked.

"Don't like that do you? Here, let's try this."

He took the drink from my hand and went to a bar, pouring more red stuff and less of the clear, strong stuff.

I took the glass from him when he offered it, and paused for a tick, just long enough to think about what I was doing. I knew it was alcohol this old man was giving me, an adult beverage, and *that* was kinda' cool. Did I like it, the taste? Maybe not so much, but I could *grow* to like it, couldn't I? For the promise of what it could do for me, that was the taste I longed for, the taste of numb, the taste of escape, *that* was the ticket. I took a drink and this time it went down *just* fine, and I was beginning to feel that disconnect. I drained the glass.

"Whoa, take it easy!" Mr. Holland said, laughing. He leaned over, looking into my somewhat glassy eyes, mirth dancing in his. "This will be our little secret, okay? Nobody needs to know, right?"

"Right!" I agreed.

"Now go finish my yard, and we'll settle up."

When I made the last cut and turned off the mower, Mr. Holland met me at the front door, handing me a five-dollar bill.

"For a job well done. Next week, same time?"

"Yes! And can I have some more of that drink when I come back?" I asked.

"Oh yes, Shannon. But remember, it's *our* secret, okay?"

"Got it, Mr. Holland!"

CHAPTER 4

I have a hereditary predisposition for alcoholism/drug abuse/addictive behaviors, given that my father was an alcoholic, so he affected my life in more negative ways than one. I spent the next week thinking about that drink, and I couldn't wait until it was time to mow Mr. Holland's yard again. This time he invited me in before I started and put a drink in my hand.

"Been looking forward to that, right?" he said with a knowing smile.

I knocked it back like a hardened boozer. It was a little stronger than the last watered-down drink he had mixed for me, almost as strong as the first one, but I didn't care. I was learning fast.

"How about another one?" I asked, batting my eyes.

"Okay," he replied, "but you gotta mow the yard, right?"

"Right. I've got it."

I finished off the second drink and started on the task at hand, not hammered but feeling tipsy. Looking back, it's a wonder I didn't cut my foot off that summer. Halfway through, I had to use the restroom, and went inside. After that, a repeat of the first time, another drink, and out the door I went to finish. He gave me the five dollars in his living room, and another mixed drink, this one not as strong.

"Can't have you falling down drunk, can we?" he said. "Listen, you don't have to wait until you mow my yard to stop by and visit," he winked.

"Okay, Mr. Holland."

I was glad to hear it.

I let two days pass before I approached Mr. Holland, spying him on his porch after school.

"Hey Shannon!" he welcomed as I walked up. "How was school?"

"Boring," I replied, rolling my eyes.

"I've got just the thing to cure that! Come on in!"

And that's the way it went for the next couple of weeks, stopping by every other day for drinks, mowing his yard on the weekends, then it was every day that I was getting my buzz on, an eleven-year-old drinking in an old man's living room.

And then one evening he said this:

"How about a game of truth or dare?"

I was half drunk at that point, maybe three quarters, and he knew it; he meted the stuff out and I guzzled it down. He dared me to pull up my shirt. I did, giggling. I thought it was funny.

"Now *you*," I slurred.

"What do you want me to do?"

"Pull down your pants."

He did so gladly, and kept them down for a while. I knew this type of behavior was forbidden, but I was fascinated by it, and being drunk I felt no shame. Before I left for home, he gave me ten dollars. My eyes widened.

"Just a gift for playing the game," he said.

There would be more games in the future.

CHAPTER 5

The visits, and the games, with Mr. Holland continued that summer. We didn't always play truth or dare, but when we did, and I showed him my body, I received money from the old pervert. And there was *always* booze. Before the end of summer and my twelfth birthday, I introduced my best friend Kristi, and another girl to Mr. Holland. I had told them he would pay for flashes, and they went along with me on a couple of occasions, giving Mr. Holland his thrills in trade for booze and money.

Mr. Holland and I never engaged in intercourse, but he took advantage of a vulnerable young girl, manipulating, touching and molesting me. In my distorted view, one that would still be so for many years to come, his attentions were evidence of his interest in me. Blinded by the need to escape my young past, having no ethical and moral father figure as my guide, I had fallen prey, under the added influence of alcohol, to Mr. Holland's evil desires. More importantly, I had no relationship with God, no inner spiritual compass to direct my heart and mind. That was not my mother's failing. She took me to church as a child. I remember hearing the sermons (but not listening to them) and standing on stage at church with my mother, singing. But my heart was frozen, and I simply could not see the cross of Christ through the blackness of the pain, anger and resentment toward my earthly father.

The daily visits continued as I entered the sixth grade. I spent most evenings at Mr. Holland's place for a couple of hours, drinking and letting him do things to me for money. I would always tell my mother that I was going over to a friend's house, and she always bought the lie. I was good at it.

One day, toward the end of the school year, I came home and there was no Mr. Holland waiting for me on his front porch. I was intercepted by my grandfather, who proceeded to inform me, shockingly, that Mr. Holland had died. My first reaction? Anger. I wasn't sad. My booze and money supply were gone. How dare he die on me!

I was in a daze, wondering what I was going to do, where was I going to go to get my mood-altering fix. I wasn't old enough to drive, let alone buy booze, but one thing was for sure: I was now a full-blown addict, and I had to have *something* to escape reality. The sober life was no longer an option for me, not after the recently deceased Mr. Holland introduced me to alcohol.

It wasn't too difficult, as it turned out. I just had to raid my grandma's medicine cabinet, which I proceeded to do, finding a bottle of Valium and helping myself. It was a different kind of high, but high just the same, and I was hooked from go.

That summer I spent the days lying out in the sun in my bathing suit, stoned on prescription drugs and all was okay in the world - not *right*, but certainly *okay*, as long as I was high.

But nothing high stays that way. The lows come, and come they would.

CHAPTER 6

A roller-skating rink in our small town was a popular destination for teens back then. My grandfather was kind enough to chauffeur Kristi and me to and from there on Saturday nights, drop off and pick up at 6:00PM and 9:00PM, respectively.

It was always packed on the weekends, lots of guys and gals, and every girl there was hot for one very cute guy in particular, a seventeen-year-old named Tony. He was also a phenomenal skater, and never missed a chance to show off in front of our dreaming eyes.

One night, Tony skated up to me quickly, grabbing the rail where I was hanging out with Kristi. A slow number had just begun playing over the rink's sound system.

"Hey, you want to dance with me?" he asked, his eyes sparkling under the strobe lights.

"Yes!" I enthusiastically replied. My eyes were sparkling too, and not just from romantic imaginings. By then I was smoking pot, supplied primarily by some friends who were bad influences. Every Saturday night Kristi and I would sneak out back and toke up before we went inside and put on our skates.

I was high as I skated in Tony's arms, and I could feel the piercing stares of jealousy from all the girls as they watched us. I felt triumphant! He had picked me over all the others!

After the song was over, we skated to the railing near the front, where Kristi was waiting for us.

"Hey, I'm starving," he said. "You want to run to Harold's with me?" Harold's was a popular burger joint in the area.

Kristi nudged an elbow softly into my side and winked.

"Sure!" I replied. I couldn't believe he was asking me to go out to eat with him. It was like a date!

"Hey, it's 7:40PM," Kristi whispered in my ear. "Make sure you're back before your grandpa comes!"

I waved her off as I walked out with Tony, beaming a great smile. They could all eat their hearts out.

He didn't talk much as he drove, and I was too shocked that I was actually with him, in his car, to speak. I stole furtive glances at his profile, and didn't notice he had passed the burger place until we were at least a half mile beyond.

"Where are we going?" I asked quietly. "You passed Harold's."

"Trust me," he said, flashing a charming smile. I melted and had no thought of protest. *Maybe he wants to park, and... kiss me*, I dared to think.

He was strangely silent as he drove off the main highway onto a dimly lit back road. I knew it led to an abandoned steam plant, where there was *no* light to speak of, and I began to feel a little nervous. There was no need to go this far off the beaten path just to park. I was a virgin still, and had no intention of changing my status this night, although I wanted to feel his lips on mine and the excitement of his touch.

He parked and sat for a moment, staring out into the darkness. I looked at him and saw his jaw muscles working, his hands gripping the steering wheel hard.

"Tony?" I whispered.

And then he turned on me, grabbing me, tearing at me like a wild animal, pulling my shirt forcefully up, his hands inside my pants.

"Wha...what are you doing?"

"Shut up!" he hissed.

"Please stop," I pled, but to no avail. I was bewildered and horrified by his animalistic aggression. Here was a good-looking guy that I so admired and couldn't wait to go with, who suddenly I wanted to be far away from.

He wouldn't stop, and he wasn't gentle. He forced himself on me and into me, burying me under him, brutally raping me as I begged for what virtue I had left, but he took it without mercy.

I checked out somewhere in the course of that experience, and came to on the side of the road where he had dumped me, abused and violated. I saw the taillights of his car disappear, and after a while, somehow, I found my bearings and got to my feet. The world swam in my vision, and I staggered to the main road. I couldn't wrap my mind around what had happened to me, couldn't begin to process it, but I had to get back to the roller rink, and that was the thought that kept me going - my grandpa would be waiting for me, and Kristi. It was a good walk back to the main road, and once there I thumbed a ride and got one. Kristi ran up to me when I arrived.

"Where have you been? It's 9:50PM!"

She was still high, and didn't even notice the blood on my clothes. Grandpa did, but said nothing to me at the time. I sat in the backseat silent, afraid to say anything. Despite what happened to me that night, I didn't want to be banned from going to the roller rink, didn't want to jeopardize losing the privileges I enjoyed. I was living with my drunken father at the time, precisely because he was a drunk and let me do whatever I wanted. He didn't care about me or what I did, and I took full advantage of it.

I told Kristi about the rape when I got home, and she was horrified.

"Are you going to be okay?" she asked, her hands clapped over her mouth, and then reaching out, pulling me into her arms. "I'm so sorry Shannon!" She cried with, and consoled me as best she could.

After she went home, I got into a hot shower and scrubbed my skin raw, washing the semen out of me, trying to rid myself of every last vestige of the horrible experience - but I could not scrub my mind clean. Everything had changed in one evening. I had had my virginity taken from me, my soul torn apart, and my heart and mind shattered.

My grandfather told my father about the blood he saw on me, and the following week, in a half sober moment, my father asked me if I had started my period. Needing to confide, and needing my father to hear me, believe me and support me for once in his miserable life and mine, I told him about the rape, how it happened, in tears.

When I was done, he didn't put an arm around my shoulder or try to comfort me. Instead, he scolded me for leaving the roller rink with a boy, and went to buy a pregnancy test. The result was negative, fortunately, but what I could not believe was this: I had told my father about a boy raping his daughter, and somehow, he was finding a way to blame *me*. I should have known from his past behavior, but I could not fathom, at that young age, that a father could be so unnaturally removed from an emotional connection to his child.

That realization, that I was raped without mercy, and blamed by my father, was not enough to drive me to God, to make me seek Him in a time of such traumatic events.

Rather, I would seek solace and escape even more so in drugs and alcohol, and my self-esteem would all but disappear.

CHAPTER 7

As terrible as the rape was, I recovered enough to function in life (with the aid of mood-altering substances).

Throughout my seventh-grade year I continued to help myself to my grandmother's pills, and score pot and alcohol from any source I could. My grandmother was older and forgetful, so she didn't miss what I took and kept getting it refilled. I took some to school and handed them out to my friends, figuring my generosity would make me cool and endear them to me. I always wanted people to like me, to want to be around me, but my methods were as misguided as my mind was.

One day someone told on me. I never knew who it was, but the gym teacher, along with the principle, opened my locker and found the pills in my coat pocket. I was suspended for six weeks, which resulted in my failing seventh grade. My mother, however furious with me initially, paid for summer school, and I was able to go on to the eighth grade.

I was leaving my childhood behind, entering eighth grade and turning thirteen. But truth be told, my childhood, already less than ideal, had been stolen from me by Mr. Holland and Tony before I arrived at the doorstep of my teen years. The calendar was merely symbolic. I would have loved to look back with rich, fond memories of my father and my family life, but that was not the case for me. I was ill prepared to face the coming years, with a warped view of what love was and the insecurity that gripped me.

But time marches ever forward, and I went with it.

CHAPTER 8

There was a rodeo that came around every year back in those days, and before the show there would be a dance in the town square. It was an opportunity for teens to mingle and meet just before the school year, and of course Kristi and I were there, dolled up and representing. After a while, a boy named Josh approached and introduced himself to me. He wasn't super cute, but he was very nice. I gave him my phone number when he asked for it, and the next night he called. He was seventeen and had a car, and he wanted to know if I could go riding around with him.

"Well, I'm just thirteen you know."

"Really? I thought you were older!"

I was suddenly afraid he would run away because of my young age.

"But I can sneak out and meet you!"

"Cool," he replied. "Just tell me when and where."

The first night we went out he was courteous, a gentleman. He took me to get something to eat, and after, when we parked, he talked to me. There was a kiss when he dropped me off, a peck on the lips, but that was it. I laid there in bed with sweet thoughts that night, hoping I had finally found someone who would be nice and treat me kindly.

But on the second date, we didn't go out to eat. He went straight to the parking and kissing, and then his hands wandered and he began touching me.

"Don't," I said, drawing in a sharp breath. The memory of the rape flashed through my mind, and he pulled back with a confused expression.

"What's wrong?"

"Nothing, I just..." I stammered, and then saw the disappointment on his face. I was desperate to be wanted, and frightened he would now leave me. "It's okay. I'm good. You got any pot?"

"Yeah, sure," he said, chuckling. "Wasn't sure you smoked."

He rolled a joint, and after a few tokes, I was relaxed and ready. This time, when he began touching me, I didn't stop him.

Into the fall and winter of that year, I continued to sneak out and meet with Josh. The sweetness of that first night was never repeated, but I clung to him, despite the fact he no longer took me out to eat or to the movies. He simply used me and I allowed it, because I needed someone to need me. I always got high before our dates, and that helped me endure.

But after the holidays he stopped coming around as often. One night, Kristi informed me she had seen Josh around town with another girl. When he finally called me, I confronted him, and at first, he tried to deny it.

"Don't know what you're talking about," he said.

"Kristi saw you with her!" I screamed.

"Whatever," he responded nonchalantly. "Listen, I'm done Shannon."

He hung up on me and that was it. I cried into my pillow for all I had given him, for all the hopes I'd held and how used I now felt.

Another male, another fail.

CHAPTER 9

I turned fourteen and entered my freshman year in high school, that point of no return. It was a time of adjustment, going to a new school building and increased learning. I had gotten over Josh (that had been ten months ago - an eternity!), but I was in no hurry for another boyfriend. My experiences with males, thus far, had not engendered in me a high opinion of that species. I mostly kept my head down and just made it through that year.

As I turned fifteen and began my sophomore year I had settled in, and felt ready to give romance a chance again. I was hoping with all my heart to meet a good guy that would take an interest in *me*.

And a month later, at a high school football game, my hopefulness was confirmed when I met Kevin, a boy unlike any I had met so far in my young life. Kristi had met a guy named Rob, and Kevin was his friend. When Kevin smiled at me, I knew I wanted to get to know him better. We spoke briefly that evening (not nearly enough for me), and when he didn't ask for my phone number, I was disappointed. He was such a nice guy! I didn't want to be too forward with him. Something about him, some aura, warned that it would be a mistake.

I learned what I could about him through Kristi, who tried to get info out of Rob. She said Rob and Kevin had been friends for about four years, and that they were involved in creative things, like making short movies, and that Kevin was a spiritual guy who came from a religious family. So that's what I had sensed about him! The quiet spirit of God was flowing through him, passed along from generations of believers down to his mother and father, and from them to him.

Rob lived in the same area of town as Kristi and me, and when he would pick up Kristi to go joyriding, I would go along, hoping Kevin might join us at some point. I asked after him, but Rob didn't seem particularly interested in talking to me about his best friend (which should have alerted me then to his intentions). Of course, Kristi knew I liked Kevin, and one day, when Rob and Kristi met with Kevin, minus me, she slipped my phone number to him.

"Give her a call," she said. "She really likes you."

"Okay, I will," Kevin responded.

I was thrilled when he called me that very night, and it was the first of many long phone conversations between us over the next several months. We learned so much about each other in those talks, and he was my first love - a romantic, a gentleman, never trying to take advantage of me, interested in and treating me with respect. It was the most beautiful, pure love I would know for many years to come.

I was still smoking pot, but not as much as I once was, and never around Kevin. My life was on an upward arc with him, but I still rode around with Rob, even without Kristi. He offered me rides, making himself constantly available to me, and he lived close by. Kevin would come to see me on occasion, and those were such wonderful times, but he lived across town, and Rob was just always there.

In the beginning, I didn't think there was anything suspicious about Rob coming by the house and giving me rides. He was Kevin's friend, and I thought he was loyal and could be trusted. But one night he tried to kiss me, and I pulled back at once, shocked and disappointed that he would betray his best friend. I asked him to take me home, and once there, I got out without another word, slamming the door. As I lay in bed, awaiting Kevin's call, I thought about telling him what had transpired, but I didn't want to cause a fissure between them.

As it turned out, I wish I had said something to Kevin that night, to save myself from the mistake I would make, to save our relationship. But I did not, and after Rob apologized and said he would never do it again, that he was wrong and misguided, I naively believed him.

Rob took his time and worked his way back, breaking down my defenses. As much as I loved Kevin, I continued going for rides with Rob and getting high.

One night Rob again tried to kiss me...and I let him.

Looking back now, I realize I was compromised by my past and addictions. I slowed down on my drug and alcohol use when I met Kevin, but could not entirely quit. Even a love like Kevin and I shared, on a deeper level than any I had known to that point in my life, was not enough to exorcise the demons of insecurity and want that dominated my thoughts. I was a slave to drugs and attention, from anyone and anywhere I could get it, chasing that elusive acceptance I would not achieve or feel until I surrendered to God.

Kevin found out about the kiss between Rob and I, and the damage was done. He no longer trusted me, and the friendship between him and Rob I worried about ending wound up ending anyway, along with the irreparable damage to Kevin and me.

That summer, toward the end of July, Kevin came back around and we got back together, sort of; but things weren't the same. He was searching for something that wasn't there anymore, not in him anyway, and I could see the distance in his eyes. We no longer talked on the phone into the early morning hours, and he didn't look at me with the same longing, the same desire. It was a deep, exquisite pain, a hurt I would feel in my heart for many years to come, that my addictions and insecurities had caused me to betray a love I held so dear. I would never forgive myself for that.

As summer turned to fall, we didn't so much break up as simply drift apart. By that time, I had already cried tears into my pillow on many nights, because I knew he was already gone.

CHAPTER 10

Almost immediately after beginning eleventh grade, I began being bullied and accosted verbally by three girls. The ringleader, whose name was Brenda, happened to be Kevin's girlfriend at the time. The other two were Alice and Kelsey, and they all made it their mission to seek me out daily, calling me vile names in front of my classmates and taunting me in the hallways and at my locker.

I knew Brenda was trying to make a point that she had and was winning Kevin, but she had no idea about the history between Kevin and me. It was an entirely pointless, mean spirited attack, and my life was sheer torture during that period. I was afraid to go to school, and I lived in constant mental agony and turmoil. I tried to tell Brenda that Kevin made up his own mind, that I was not in his life, that she had nothing to fear, but nothing I could say or do would stop her.

Mine was a case of extreme bullying that went unchecked. This was in a time before bullying received it's just due as an egregious offense, and I had no one to help me. It was one of the most horrific periods of my life, and although I was no fighter I knew, when the time came, what I had to do.

That opportunity presented itself when Brenda and her friends showed up at my house one day, out in the street, daring me to come outside and fight. I was plenty afraid and certain I would lose, but I also understood that if I didn't go out there, the bullying would continue. I summoned all the courage I could and went out to confront her. I was beaten down quickly. I was no fighter, had never even *been* in a fight, and when they finally left, I staggered back into the house, one eye swollen shut and my body hurting all over. I collapsed on the bed and stared at the ceiling (through my one good eye), and thought about where I was now. I hoped today would mark the end of Brenda and company's torment, and thankfully, that would prove to be true.

There was no going back, no mending Kevin's and my relationship. I had made sure of that, and the resulting heartbreak and bitterness of losing my chance at true love (what I thought then would be my *only* chance), and the misery of the attacks by Brenda, had caused me to step up my drug use to unprecedented levels.

I had stood at a crossroads and chosen the wrong path, one that would take me deeper into self-destruction. What sense of worth I had going into my relationship with Kevin was now gone.

My heart was growing ever colder as I weighed what life had in store for me. Why bother being emotional, when all it brought was pain? No matter the cause and effect, whose fault it was, love just hurt in the end. I decided right then and there to seal my heart shut. There would be nothing to rival what I had lost, so I would do drugs and lose myself in the world until my pain was gone or forgotten.

CHAPTER 11

With purposeful abandon and dark thoughts ruling my heart and mind, I fell in with a girl I met at the roller rink in my sixteenth year. She was bold and strong, and I liked that about her, so opposite the meek, insecure person I had always been. She was what I wanted to be now, a person with no regard for other's opinions or need to be loved.

She also knew where to buy drugs, pot in particular. My mother had recently bought a car for me, and I would drive her around to the dealers she knew.

One Saturday night none of the regulars had any pot to sell, so we drove to the next town over, but no one had anything there either.

"Hey, let's go to the city, to the projects there. I'm sure I'll know somebody," my new friend suggested.

"Okay, sure," I agreed readily. Although I was driving, I was just along for the ride. She was the dominate one, but as long as I got the drugs to get high, everything was cool.

I drove up to one of the buildings and parked curbside.

"I'll be back in a minute, okay?" she said, climbing out of my car.

"Okay, be careful!" I advised.

She was gone for a few minutes, and as I sat there alone in the driver's seat, I looked around nervously. This was a very bad part of town, a high crime area. After what seemed like forever, she reappeared with three African American men in tow. They looked at me as my new friend opened the back door and grabbed a manila envelope, which contained modeling pictures we had just picked up that day. They had been taken by a photographer in the county, and although there were no nudes, there were some bathing suit shots of both of us.

"What are you doing?" I whispered shrilly.

"It's all good Shannon," she replied, winking, and I could tell she had already taken a hit with these guys. "I'm just gonna show our pictures to them. Relax." I stayed where I was as the three men ogled our pictures; then she came around to my window.

"Hey, they've invited us inside. Come on," she waved.

She had a thing for African American men and, like everything else, she wasn't shy about it.

"Why don't you just pay them, get the drugs and go?" I suggested.

One of the men stepped up to the window.

"Hey, it's cool. We just want to smoke up with y'all."

"Free drugs!" My new friend whispered.

Nothing's free, I thought, and against a fleeting moment of better judgment, I got out of the car and went in with them.

We all took a seat on a ragged sectional, and the leader of the pack lit a bong pipe, took a draw and passed it around. It was strong stuff, and in short order I was very high. I saw my friend get up and go into another room with one of them.

She likes it, I thought.

"What about you?" one of the remaining two asked, smiling and leaning forward into my face. He had two shiny gold teeth.

Did I say that out loud?

"Yeah, you did," he replied.

Boy was I stoned!

The next thing I knew I was being dragged by this gold-toothed man into a restroom, where he proceeded to lock the door and rape me. I was powerless against his assault, due both to my small size and level of inebriation. When he was done, he left and the other one came in and helped himself to me. This continued most of the night, as they took turns brutally raping me.

"We got your keys, your car and your money," one informed me at some point. "You're going to be a slave for us now."

My new friend, I assumed, was also enduring sexual assault, but I wasn't so sure she wasn't consenting. As for me, it was horrible. I had not been so violated since Tony raped me and put me out on the side of the road.

In the morning the leader of the pack, for some reason, decided to let us go. He took me aside.

"Listen, that girlfriend of yours done told us everything," he said. "Where you live, where your mama lives. If you tell anyone what we did I swear we'll kill your family. Understand?"

With that threat, he gave me my car keys (but kept my money) and shoved us both out the door. He meant what he said, I was sure. Once back in the car, I turned on this new friend and screamed, "Why did you tell them where my mom lives?"

"They were going to kill me!" she shot back. "You would have done the same thing."

She was a little too nonchalant about it.

"They raped me!" I cried.

"Me too!" she replied, "But we can't do anything about it, Shannon! They'll kill us all if we talk. If we stay quiet, there won't be any trouble."

She was right, I knew. They were guilty of a terrible crime, and no one would ever know. They would never have to pay for what they did.

The experience was devastating. I had lived a way beyond Mr. Holland and Tony, and had even had a brief moment of promise, of a cleaner, more honest life. From that wreckage I ran to drugs and to a friendship with this new person in my life, which led to further abhorrent violation of my body and person.

I couldn't see that back then. I was blind to the truth, and my heart simply grew colder and harder as a result of that gang rape. The Shannon I had been just a year before was dying, fading away, being replaced by a hardened version, emotionally cold and mentally tough. It was drugs I needed, always, and I was going to get them anyway I could. I needed them to survive, to deal with all of the bad that would take over my mind if I let it.

I was not going to allow that to happen.

CHAPTER 12

I somehow managed to graduate high school, and it was due in no small part to my mother's influence. The hair salon she opened a few years before had become quite a success in our small town, and most of my teachers were clients of hers. I know I did not apply myself to my studies, or make good grades in my drug induced haze. Still, I walked across the stage and received my diploma, proud to be among my classmates.

I had continued hanging out with my new friend (who I will now refer to as Trigger} after that awful night in the city. She helped me get the drugs I so needed, and that's all that mattered to me. My mother knew about Trigger's bad reputation through her clients at the hair salon and she regularly berated me about her.

"You need to stop hanging around with that slut, Shannon!" she yelled at me one night, not long after graduation.

I was painting my toe nails, ignoring her as best I could. I knew where this was going. I thought: *Here it comes: You still live under my roof young lady...*

"You still live under my roof young lady!" {She continued right on cue.) "And I'm paying for that car you use to pick her up and go do God knows what!"

"We're not doing anything *bad* Mom," I lied. I was high at that moment. She had no clue.

"Not doing anything bad?" she scoffed. "Maybe not you, not *yet*, but if you keep hanging around a girl like that, you're going to get in trouble, Shannon. Everybody, and I mean *everybody*, knows what a whore she is. Why do you want to hang around with someone like that? It's embarrassing me!"

And I didn't care, not in the least.

"Are you done?" I asked, screwing the cap on my nail polish.

"Yeah, I'm done," she replied, steel in her voice. "I'm done paying for that car you drive, done letting you drive it."

"What?" She had my attention now. "You can't take my car..."

"It's not *your* car Shannon! I make the payments and pay the insurance! You don't have a job!"

"I've been looking!" I shot back.

She came and sat in front of me, on the loveseat, collecting herself. "Shannon, there's a client of mine that is a supervisor at Cress Insurance in the city," she informed me. "She says she can get you on there."

"Really?"

I knew it was a good company to work for, and they paid well, even entry level positions.

"But you have to straighten up, Shannon. This is an opportunity for you to fly right. Do you want the job? It's that or lose the car."

Not much of a choice there, but I actually *did* want to try it. If I could make it work, maybe it would lead to other paths. I wasn't thinking about quitting drugs, but maybe I could balance a professional life and a partying life. It was worth a try.

I got the job and did well there for a while, going to work at Cress Monday through Friday, meeting new people, and not smoking dope during the day. I was seeing less of Trigger, but we still got together on the weekends, unbeknownst to my mom. One Saturday night, while we were out running around, she directed me to this guy in the projects. I thought we were going to buy pot, but the dealer pulled a clear bag with white powder from his coat pocket.

"What's that?" I inquired.

"Cocaine," Trigger replied, her eyes dancing. "It's great stuff!" She turned to the dealer. "Can we come inside and take a hit? It's her first time."

"Sure. Got the money, right?" he asked.

"Yes!" she answered, and then turned to me. "Right Shannon?"

I rolled my eyes. Trigger, the moocher, *never* had money.

"Yeah. Have you done this before?" I asked.

"Yes, and you'll love it, just wait!"

And love it I did. I had stood at another crossroads and chosen another wrong path, with Trigger pulling me along. I could not see it then, but that girl wasn't doing me any favors. And it wouldn't be the last time my association with her led me places I may not have gone on my own. Not excusing myself, of course. I chose to hang out with her.

So now I had a new drug, cocaine, and it was expensive, costing way more than pot. But I had to have it. No going back.

After that night, we scored cocaine every weekend, free basing it, but my job didn't pay enough to keep up with my powerful new addiction. I needed more money, and I began doing things that I wouldn't have thought about before, like stealing from my drunken dad, all for the sake of that amazing high. I would simply wait for him to pass out and write myself a check for cash. They knew me and my family at a local grocery store, and would readily cash the checks I brought in, five hundred dollars at a time. No big deal.

I kept that little thieving operation up successfully, and one weekend, Trigger told me about this truck driver she met who wanted us to move in with him. He lived in a mobile home, just across the state line, and he was gone a lot.

"So we can party all we want!" she exclaimed. "He'll never know! I'm sure he doesn't care anyway."

"It'll take me a lot longer to get to work!" I argued, but Trigger convinced me to do it, as she always did. Mother wasn't happy about my moving out, but I packed up and went with Trigger to some guy's home who partied all the time.

The train was rolling on a downward stretch, and I was on board, entirely unaware of where I was going.

CHAPTER 13

I was in training at Cress Insurance, and managed to keep my job for the first two months, even as I free based cocaine almost daily after work with Trigger and around the clock on the weekends.

Everything was one big happy time until my grandpa, who balanced my dad's checkbook and paid his bills, was notified by the bank that one of my dad's checks had bounced. On further investigation he found it was I who wrote it, and he proceeded to call my mother, who proceeded to call me.

This was a time before cell phones, and, apparently, I had given mother the number to the mobile home where I was living at some point. I was pretty much stoned out of my mind when she called me on a Saturday evening.

"Shannon?"

"Yes?"

"Why are you writing checks for cash using your father's account?"

"What? Who is this?" The radio was on, loud, and I strung the chord into the next room.

"Are you there Shannon?"

"Mom?"

"Yes, it's your mom! Are you asleep?"

"No, I'm...what's up?"

"You've been writing checks for cash from your dad's account, over two thousand dollars so far!" she screamed. "Where's that money Shannon? What are you doing..."

I hung up on her. Busted! There went my money supply to buy drugs! That was my first thought as an addict; no shame or embarrassment, just selfishness. The phone rang three or four more times before she gave up.

I had stocked up on drugs for the weekend, and on Sunday I started extra early. As every addict knows, dire situations are added incentive to use a bit more, just something extra to help ease your mind, calm your nerves. By the time my mom and step father pulled up outside, I was high as a kite in a good March wind.

"Who's that?" some guy said, staring out the kitchen window. I didn't know half the people who wandered in and out of the place. I slid over, looking out the window, and my eyes, almost slits a moment before, opened wide in surprise.

"Oh crap, it's my mom!" I shrieked. How did they find this place? "Shh! Everybody quiet!" I whispered, waving them down.

Trigger and some guy she was with looked at me, perplexed, as did everyone else in the room before my mom began pounding on the door.

"Shannon, open up! I know you're in there!"

"Who is that?" Trigger asked.

"My mom! Don't answer the door anybody!"

"Shannon, come out and talk to us!" my mom implored. But I was too scared, too high and too paranoid to even consider it. I ran to the back bedroom and closed the door.

After a while she stopped knocking and imploring, and I rose off the bed, peeking out a window on the same side as the driveway. I saw my step father in their car, and my mom was...in *my* car? She was taking my car! I ran out of the bedroom and slammed on the brakes at the front door. What could I do? She had me.

"She's taking your car, huh?" the guy, who I didn't know and was still staring out the kitchen window, said. "That sucks."

It did. What was I going to do now? I couldn't face my mother, now that she knew I had stolen from Dad, and all of the questions that would follow. In the subsequent days, rather than call her and talk about it, and ask forgiveness, I just sat in the trailer, getting rides here and there. As I had no transportation or way of getting to work, I lost my job at Cress Insurance.

A week later, it was Trigger to the rescue again.

"Hey, I know this guy in New York. He's a trick," she said.

"What's a trick?" I'd never heard that term.

"Shannon, I *swear*," she replied, rolling her eyes. "He's an old guy, name's Louie; he's about eighty or something, all alone. He'll give us a place to live, feed us and give us money. All we have to do is give him sex every now and then. He'll die soon anyway."

Well, I had done that before, hadn't I? Sounded like Mr. Holland II. And at this point, what did it matter? I had lost my job and my car. There was nothing left for me in Tennessee.

"How do we get to New York?" I asked.

Trigger smiled.

CHAPTER 14

"Hey, I've found a trucker who'll help us get to New York," Trigger informed me a few days later. "He can get us halfway there, and he knows some other truckers that have routes the rest of the way. So, we've got the rides!"

"When do we leave?" I asked.

"Thursday."

Two days. After a wild, tumultuous summer, I would be leaving my home state, preferring to run to New York than face my mother's disappointment and questions. I had no idea what awaited me, but I knew what I was leaving behind: a mess of things, a mess of my life. I would be high all the time in New York, the same as in Tennessee, but at least I wouldn't be reminded daily of my traumatic years in the small town where I had spent my life; where I was molested as a child, raped as a young teen and in love as a young woman, everything I had lost.

We arrived at the parking lot and climbed into the trucker's cab. He was a middle aged, totally unattractive white man with a large beer gut, wearing an undersized tee shirt.

"Well hello girls," he said, flashing a semi toothless smile.

"This is Shannon," Trigger introduced.

"Hello, Ladies just call me, Big Daddy Trucker. Glad to have ya on board," he said, and then parted the curtain that separated the sleeping area from the cab. "You first," he said, pointing a chubby finger at Trigger. As he went through the curtain I grabbed her arm.

"What is this? What's going on?" I whispered.

"You didn't think we were going to ride for free, did you?"

"I'm not sleeping with *that*," I stated, pointing at the curtain and curling my nose.

"You will if you want to get to New York. Look, it's no big deal. Just think about something else."

And when it came my turn to lay under him, I took her advice. It was disgusting, but I endured it for the sake of making it to New York. When we were handed off to another trucker in Virginia, we had to again pay for our ride with sex; but it was easier this time, as I was becoming desensitized with the exposure, able to disconnect myself from the act. It helped that Trigger had negotiated pot for us as part of the deal. It was so much easier to do when high.

On that trip we had sex with every trucker that helped us to our destination. I would call it the beginning of my career as a prostitute, but it actually began with Mr. Holland seven years earlier. That hadn't been to the point this was, sexual intercourse, but the premise was established then: my body, a view, a touch, in exchange for money or services rendered.

It was a natural progression downward for me at that point in my life. I had no sense of self-worth, and I had grown colder as time passed and my drug use increased.

I would now arrive in New York hardened and ready to *really* do anything to get the drugs I needed.

CHAPTER 15

Trigger and I finally arrived at the old man's home in New York, two girls barely out of high school embarking on a new journey. Life there consisted of our providing Louie with sex on occasion (he wasn't too randy at his age), and he, in turn, gave us spending money, which we used to buy drugs. The drugs were more expensive in New York, however, and despite our requests for more money, the old man wouldn't budge.

"I'm giving you a roof over your head, feeding you, giving you good money, I'm not giving you anymore!" Louie exclaimed, waving a gnarled finger at us.

So, Trigger, always hustling, found work for us at a strip joint. I had no idea what I was doing, but I learned on the go. You chose your outfits out of this big pile, but it was your responsibility to launder and keep up with them.

The club did a thriving business off the apparently sex starved men of New York, and Trigger and I both made lots of money. We blew it all on drugs of course, and to make extra money we began meeting clients after work, prostituting. We were caught in the cyclone, and one night, Trigger was in the wrong place at the wrong time. She was arrested, swept up in a drug sting, and suddenly my partner in crime was gone, leaving me alone with the old man.

Louie would take me to work, and I continued to provide him with sex, all for the drugs. And as much trouble as I got into with Trigger over the years, she was the only friend I had, the one that had my back. I was rudderless and adrift without her, so when Jimmy Givazio, an Italian man who had been expressing interest in me beyond that of a stripper and client, approached me again one night, I was open.

"Listen, you don't have to do this," he told me. He wasn't good looking, not at all; but he had money - and *drugs*. "You'll never want for anything, baby. And you'll have all the coke you want, okay? I'm a dealer! I don't use myself, but I've got lots of clients. Come stay with me."

So, I did. That very night I walked out of the strip club with him, and he whisked me away to his large, upscale home in the suburbs.

It would be three years before I would emerge.

CHAPTER 16

1987:

Ronald Reagan was three years into his second term as President, Whitney Houston was still alive and belting out "How Will I Know?" on the radio, and I was eighteen years old, beginning my three-year imprisonment at the home of Jimmy Givazio, a clean and sober drug dealer who kept me as his personal sex slave and made sure I was consistently stoned out of my mind.

Jimmy was dealer to the wealthy suburbanites as well as major bands when they came to New York. He would parade me around in front of his guests on some of these occasions, his trophy girl, and I met some of the top acts of the day, although I was too drugged to remember much about them or those times. I was always high. Jimmy knew I was a hopeless addict and he made sure I had an endless supply of drugs; his aim, of course, to keep me right where he wanted me: a mindless servant to him, and that I was.

When he wasn't parading me around or having sex with me, he often found an excuse to physically and verbally assault me. He had a viciously bad temper, and I endured it all for the drugs.

The weeks and months passed and I drifted in a fog, no concept of time, days blending together. There was Jimmy and dope, dope and beatings, dope and Jimmy and beatings, the wheel went round and round.

Although I was never in want of drugs, I missed having someone to share the high with. Jimmy had no desire for drugs or drink; money was his high. Occasionally, a client would ask to get high with me.

"Go ahead," Jimmy would say, smiling, anything to please a customer and make more money. So, these people would sit with me and we would get our thing on, talking and laughing. It was an experience I looked forward to, and I would eagerly answer the door in hopes it would be one of my "get high" friends.

By the time I opened the door and the police came pouring in to arrest me and Jimmy Givazio, it was 1989 and I was twenty years old. When they put me in the back of the squad car and drove away, it was the first time I had been outside of Jimmy's house since I arrived three years earlier.

CHAPTER 17

"Your Honor, she had nothing to do with the drugs," Jimmy stated magnanimously to the court the next day at our hearing. "It was my business, I controlled everything. She had no idea what I was doing."

I was shocked. This guy, who never missed a chance to degrade or physically abuse me over the last three years, was letting me off the hook and shouldering all the blame?

The court released me on his testimony, and the first thing I did was head back to Jimmy's house, where I hoped I would find the drugs I had hidden. I had the shucks and jives, needing a fix badly.

I had to grab a chair to reach the cabinet over the fridge, and when I opened the canister... pay dirt.

I made my fix, a strong dose (the classic more than you need when you want it so bad), with trembling hands at the kitchen table. When it kicked in, I began floating, and when Jimmy stormed into the kitchen, I was comfortably numb. He had bonded out not long after I left, and was now in a perfect rage. He backhanded me viciously, knocking me out of the chair onto the floor.

"Why did you open the door, b***h?" he screamed. "Why did you let the police in? I would have had time to flush it!"

I tried to crawl away. I knew what was coming, and I was honestly thankful I had taken a higher dose. It would spare me some of the pain.

He got a death grip on my hair and hauled me to my feet, turning my eyes to his. He was *crazy* mad.

"You're high, aren't you? Had some squirreled away? Look at you, you useless stoned b***h!"

And with that, he slammed me into a sliding glass door. It broke and I went through, a shard of glass slashing my wrist open on the way. I lay there, pretending I was out, and Jimmy stalked off. I would later go to the hospital, after wrapping my wound and sobering up some, and they would work on my injury; but the nerve damage was extensive, and to this day I cannot move or bend the middle finger of my right hand.

I went back to Jimmy's and somehow made it through that window of time before he went away. My hidden stash ran out quickly, and there was no way for me to sneak out and secure drugs. I went through some awful days, and none worse than the day before he went to prison.

In the kitchen he grabbed me by my hair and held my face close to a hot stove eye, turned up full heat. I could feel it beginning to bake my face as he threatened me.

"B***h, I'm going to prison for two years!" he shouted. "You better be working, taking care of this house and sending me money, you got it?"

"Yes! I promise!" I agreed emphatically.

I agreed to all of it, just to pacify him, and get my face away from that hot stove eye.

And the next day, off to prison he went.

CHAPTER 18

After Jimmy went to the pen, I tried to get my old stripper job back, but they wouldn't rehire me because I had quit without notice and left with a client. I needed money for drugs, but I didn't want to resort to prostitution again, not so soon after my three-year ordeal with Jimmy. The promise I made to Jimmy about making his house payments and sending him money was a bald-faced lie. I had no intention of ever seeing that hateful, evil man again (but you know what they say about intentions).

So, I set about selling and pawning everything in his house I could, and the money I made bought my drugs for a while. I had not needed a drug dealer over the past three years, but in order to feed my addiction, I now had to find one. I discovered a pusher who dealt drugs through a hole in his first-floor screen window. You knocked on the window, he would slide it up, and the exchange was made.

One night when I arrived, an older guy was standing around close to the window. He looked suspicious, and I was duly wary, but I was jonesing so bad I went ahead and approached, wadding my money and sticking it in the hole. As soon as my hand closed on the package the stranger grabbed me by the throat, attempting to strangle me and drag me away, no doubt with the intention of raping me. I managed to kick him in the family jewels, however, and he released me. I took off, but the old guy, remarkably, was giving chase and hot on my heels. *Must not have gotten a direct hit on him*, I thought, but there was little time to think as he was gaining. I spied a tree with low limbs and scrambled up like a monkey.

He stopped below the tree, hands on his knees, breathing hard. He was too old to climb and get to me.

"What's wrong, creep?" I hollered.

"I'll get you," he panted. "You have to come down sometime."

Great, I thought. I didn't know how long he could or would wait, but I needed my fix, so I lit up, perched in a tree.

He finally left, and I crept down the tree, on the lookout until I made it back home safely.

As fall faded to the snowy winters of New York I ran out of things to sell, and the house, after several missed payments, was foreclosed on. I had to vacate the premises, and I took to the street, living in a shelter for the homeless. I wanted my drugs, but still wasn't willing to prostitute myself again to get them. I could get a job, but for what? To buy drugs, and then I'd lose the job at some point, so what *was* the point? I had to decide - I didn't have money enough to feed my addiction for more than two days. I was torn, lonely and frightened.

Even though I had gone through experiences by then that would be enough trouble to last a lifetime, I was still only twenty years old. I was young enough to do something with my life, to change direction, and after three years of zero communication I broke down and called my mother.

"Shannon, is that really *you*?" she squealed into the phone.

"Yes, Mom, I'm so sorry..."

I sobbed uncontrollably, the weight of all I had been through crashing down on me. I told her everything I could.

"Shannon, listen to me. It doesn't matter *what* you've done. I thought you were dead! Where are you right now?"

"New York," I responded.

"I'll book a flight home for you tonight! Oh, Shannon honey, don't worry about anything! Everything's going to be alright, okay?"

"Thanks Mom," I cried.

I rang off, and that night I boarded a flight back home to Tennessee. As I sat next to the window, flying above the clouds, I pondered what would be next for me. I knew my mom would probably put me in rehab, and I was willing to go, to give it a shot. I had called her, hadn't I? That was going to be the deal, but I was so afraid of sobriety, of living with my past in my head, nothing to buffer the thoughts and quiet the demons.

But now I had to try.

CHAPTER 19

The reunion with my mother was an emotional, tearful occasion. True to her word she didn't bring up the past, but rehab came up quickly.

"Now Shannon, I am willing to help you but you have to help yourself. I think the sooner we get you into a program the better. Don't you?"

"Sure," I replied, with not much enthusiasm, and she noticed.

"Now, you have to *want* to do this for it to work, Shannon."

"I know Mom! I'm just tired."

I went in for the standard thirty days, and it was wonderful while I was in, but that almost utopian, structured, peaceful lifestyle is not real world, and when I came out, the memories flooded back into my mind - the life I had lived, the things I had done, the life I had lost. But it works if you work it, that's what they say. Question was: How was *I* going to make it work?

Next: Employment. An idle mind is the devil's workshop, as the old saying goes, so I got a job at a local grocery store as a cashier. A good ole' friend from high school named Cheri worked there, she was drop dead gorgeous and we had known each other well in school, we struck up a conversation. She lived with the Store Manager, and he threw parties at his house most Saturday nights. I had not told Cheri anything about my life in New York, my addiction to drugs and rehab, so she had no reservations about inviting me to party. I did not trust myself early on, so I politely turned her down the first few times. Ultimately, the pressure was too much and I went with her one Saturday night.

When offered a beer, I took it, and when the golden liquid touched my lips, it was the first mood-altering substance to enter my body in almost a year. I nursed it most of the evening, so I hardly felt any effect. I could smell pot, but I stayed away from those groups, and I begged off early when I felt the temptation to have another drink coming on. I wasn't sure I could handle just drinking, that consumption of alcohol wouldn't lead me back to pot and then to the hard drugs.

Gradually, however, over the next couple of months, I found I could have a couple of drinks at a local bar or at a party, get a good buzz on socially and be okay with that. My confidence increased, and the thought that I could lead a normal life began to be more than just fantasy. I began to dream, for the first time since Kevin, about finding love again.

One night, at the bar, I was approached by a handsome guy who had been popular in high school.

"Hey, you're Shannon, right?" he said, smiling.

"Yes!" I confirmed. I couldn't believe he was talking to me.

"I'm Brad."

"I know."

Cheri appeared behind him, flashing a big smile and thumbs up.

"You graduated in...?"

"Nineteen- eighty- six," I finished.

"What have you been doing since school?"

"Oh, just working, you know. What about you? What do you do?"

"I work at the Coca-Cola plant," he replied.

 Handsome? Check. Good job? Check.

"So, you want to go get something to eat?"

"Yes!" I readily agreed.

I felt almost like a normal person again, walking out of that bar on a summer evening, going on a date with a good-looking guy. I could smell fresh mown grass, and the sky was purplish in the twilight of the day. New York and Jimmy were light years away, another life, another world. It was time to make this work, to settle down. I had proven I could do it over the last year. There were no drugs in my system. I was clean.

Brad and I grabbed a bite, and then he grabbed a bottle of tequila at the liquor store. He suggested we go to his place, and I agreed, filled with anticipation. The evening felt magical so far, and I hoped it would lead to more. At his apartment, we sat on the couch and did shots, and then kissed. It felt so good, so romantic, the way it did when Kevin and I kissed. My head swimming, lost in the moment and the memories, the two places in time melding together, I let him touch me, undress me and make love to me.

I had driven my mom's car to Brad's apartment, so when I awoke the next morning, he was gone. He left a note saying he had to go to work, and I left one for him with my phone number on it.

I went home and hung around the house that evening, expecting him to call me.

But he didn't.

Or the next day. Or the next.

I was bitterly disappointed that Brad had not called me by the time I went to the bar with Cheri on Saturday night. I wouldn't speak to him if I saw him, but I wanted to show up and let him know I was okay. I wasn't, of course. I was devastated. Granted, I had put too much into one evening with a guy, but those evenings had been so few in my life and my expectations had been so great. I had been ready, so ready, for love and commitment. I had been in a good place in my mind; all I needed was a partner, someone to help me.

He didn't show up that night, as it turned out, and I proceeded to throw caution to the wind and get blind drunk. It was the first of several desperate moments I would feel in the coming weeks, moments that would weaken and test my resolve.

CHAPTER 20

I went to work at the grocery store over the next two weeks, just going through the motions.

"Hey, we're having a party at the house this Saturday night!" Cheri announced, and I looked at her glumly. "You need *something* to cheer you up! He's cute, but he ain't all that! Get over it, girl!"

"I know, I know," I sighed. "It's okay, Cheri. I'll be there."

"Good!"

The night of the party, Cheri intercepted me in the driveway, handing me a beer. After clinking our bottles together and toasting the evening ahead, she produced a bottle of Percocet that she'd been prescribed for her recent oral surgery.

"These will give you a kick," she said with a wink, and I knew they would. They were drugs, the legal kind, but drugs still. I hesitated, knowing where this could lead, but I was in too much pain again. I hadn't been in love with *Brad*, just the *idea* of being in love. With the crushing of that idea, all of the insecurity, resentment and pain that

I hoped to erase had come back full force in my fragile mind.

"Give me," I said, tapping out four of them and chasing them down with a swig of beer.

"Whoa!" Cheri exclaimed. "You want to stay on your feet, girl!"

"I don't care. Let's party."

"You okay?" Cheri asked, concern on her face, and I nodded. My tongue was too thick to speak. There were guys paying attention to me, popular football players I recognized from high school days. They were smiling and flirting with me, and when I saw Brad across the room looking my way, I became animated, reaching out to the closest male and draping myself all over him, all the while checking Brad, making sure he was seeing this, how wanted I was!

I blacked out for a bit. Then...

Back. There was a hand holding mine, leading me into a room. What? I think I was giggling.

Black out.

I came to and there was a guy on top of me.

"Mitchell?" I heard laughs, and a guy came out of the closet holding a video camera, filming us having sex.

"What?" I screamed. The drugs had worn off, enough so that I was aware of what was happening. "Get off of me!"

He rolled off, and I got up, pulling my clothes on. "Give me that camera!"

But the guy filming, who happened to be one of the popular football players, had skipped out of the room. I would never get my hands on that video, I knew. I left the party in shame, tears burning my eyes as I ran out of the house.

CHAPTER 21

Ten months had passed since I left New York, and until I downed the Percocet I had not so much as touched a single drug. Now I wanted more, especially after the sex video was shown around. I was so embarrassed, and after the one night and done with Brad and the rape video (which it was - I was drugged and did not consent) I was ready to get out of town, far away; but how to make it happen? I didn't have any money to speak of. And that's when the phone rang, and I answered and heard the voice of Jimmy Givazio.

"Hey, baby, it's Jimmy! How you doing?"

"Jimmy? You're out of jail?" My heart was pounding. *I must have given him this phone number at some point,* I thought, *and now he's out, early, has to be, it hasn't been two years, and good God he is going to find me and kill me for sure!* (I had forgotten he plead out, and only got 12 months in jail.)

"Yeah, baby!" he replied, sounding cheerful for some reason. "I got out for good behavior!"

Good behavior? Not the Jimmy *I* knew!

"Well...that's great!" I lied. He didn't *sound* mad, so I played along.

"I know what you're thinkin' babe. You're thinkin' I'm upset about the house and my stuff right? Well, I'm not. You did what you had to do. I completely understand."

"You do?" I asked, incredulous.

"Yeah! I would a done the same thing, truly. I don't care about any of that stuff anyway, it's *you* I love baby. I'm sorry about all the bad stuff I did to you, really."

Was he serious? He didn't sound like the same man. Maybe prison *had* changed him.

"So how about it? I'd love to see you," he said.

"What are you talking about?"

"I'll fly you up here, babe. I promise it will be okay this time, I'll make it right. And I'm dealing again. I have drugs."

Bingo! That was all he needed to say. I couldn't use here, but I could there. Before Brad, the party and the video (and the Percocet), I would have never agreed to return to Jimmy and New York and drugs.

But now I couldn't *wait* to go back.

CHAPTER 22

My mother overheard (eavesdropped on) my conversation with Jimmy, and when I hung up, she was in my face.

"Was that who I think it was?"

"Leave me alone Mom." She had been nagging me lately about staying out late, suspicious of my every move. She had reason to be, I suppose, but she had no idea how humiliated I was or how ready I was to blow this town.

"You're not...you're not thinking about going *back* to him are you?" she stammered. "Shannon, you've worked so hard! Why throw it all away?"

I ignored her and went to my room, pulling a bag out of the closet, the same one I had come home with fourteen months ago, and began packing. I had no idea how I was going to get to the airport, but get there I would. I couldn't stay here, or in a sober state of mind, anymore.

"Shannon, I can't let you do this," my mother stated with authority as she stood in the doorway watching me pack.

"I'm going, Mom," I replied, my jaw set determinedly. "You have no idea."

"Then explain it to me!" she shrieked.

"I can't Mom," I replied, exasperated. "It's my life, okay?"

She threw her hands up and stalked off.

When I entered the living room with my bag over my shoulder, I saw my step sister Vickie had arrived.

"Where are you going Shannon?" my mom asked.

"To the airport."

"How are you going to get there?"

"I'll hitch if I have to."

"I'm not going to let you go," she said, with certainty.

"You can't stop me," I said, with more certainty.

My friend was watching all of this intently.

"Well, I would love to stay and chat, but I have a plane to catch," I said; but when I got to the door, my mother blocked me.

"Move, Mom," I demanded, but she wouldn't budge.

The frustration of the past few weeks rose like molten lava inside of me and I exploded in rage.

"Move Mom!" I shouted, and pushed her, with a surge of strength, out of the way. She fell to the floor and looked up at me, shocked.

I was breathing hard, glaring at her. "Don't even *think* about trying to stop me again," I seethed.

Vickie came up to me, grabbing my arm. "Come on, let's go."

"What?"

"I'll take you to the airport, if you want to go that bad."

Mom was crying as I left, but my heart was once again cold, and I welcomed the emotional disconnect.

CHAPTER 23

When I arrived in New York, I took a cab to a motel where Jimmy was staying. When he opened the door and greeted me, I noticed he appeared thinner.

"Shannon," he said simply. No kiss, or hug, or "Hello baby." "Come on in."

I sat my bag on a chair by the lone table in the room and turned toward him.

"Is this oka.." and he hit me with his balled fist, right in the nose. Blood spurted out as I fell back on the bed, but he wasn't done, not by a long shot. He grabbed me by the hair of the head (one of his favorite moves,) and pulled my face to his.

"You stupid b***h!" he shouted. "You fell for it! You're going to pay for what you did, letting my house go, selling my stuff!"

He proceeded to kick and slap me around, and thankfully, the only thing broken in that conflict was my nose.

"And I don't have any drugs for you, either," he said after administering the punishment, laughing cruelly. "I can't deal in that stuff for a while. I'm going to work for a trucking company."

I groaned inside. He was right about one thing: I was stupid, stupid enough to fall for his lies. Now I was up here, his slave again, and no drugs to ease my mental and (with him) physical pain.

He had not had a woman in fourteen months, and he sexually assaulted me, even as I lay there bleeding, taking care of himself with no mind for me. But it was nothing new; it had been that way for most of my life.

The cold was settling deeper into my heart and mind. I determined right then and there that this time around, I wasn't going to mentally curl into the fetal position. He could beat me, but I was going to play it smart and make it work for me somehow.

A week later, the first day he went back to his job, I went out and found one of my old connections and got stoned. I made it back to the hotel before Jimmy got home, but he could tell I was high, and that earned me a slap.

"So you went out and found some, huh?" he spat, but I didn't cower and I looked at him evenly.

"Yes, I did. I know it's not your thing, Jimmy, but it's mine."

He studied me for a moment, seemingly trying to decide whether to hit me again or not. He chose the latter, and actually smiled.

"Okay," he said, nodding. "You're not going anywhere, right?"

"Why would I?" I said, shrugging my shoulders and smiling. Of course, as he fell for my acting job, I was planning my escape. I didn't intend to stay with Jimmy. There would come a time, an opportunity, and I would bolt.

Before long, Jimmy rented an apartment. After that initial beating, he calmed down some and life was okay. It was the opening I had been looking for.

One day, after he went to work, I packed a bag and left. My destination was a girlfriend I had found, a student at Empire State who lived in a nice apartment off campus, compliments of Daddy's money. Said money also purchased drugs for Daddy's girl, who shared them with me. I met her as we were both purchasing from the same dealer, and we struck up a conversation. She had told me about her classmates, how they were prudes, and she had no one to get high with. After a couple of visits, I played on her sympathies with my story of being held hostage by Jimmy, how he beat and assaulted me.

It worked. She practically begged me to escape and stay with her.

So, there I was, and the feeling of freedom and new beginnings lasted about forty-eight hours.

It seemed Jimmy still had connections around town. He sent a couple of guys to find me, and, while my new friend was gone to school and I was sitting around getting high, the goons broke into the room and hauled me out, back to Jimmy's apartment. They didn't tie me up, but made sure I stayed put until he got home.

When he arrived, he didn't go berserk, strangely. He dismissed his hired hands and took a seat across from me at the kitchen table, folding his hands. I was immediately suspicious.

"I thought you were happy," he said, and I actually saw *pain* in his eyes. Did this guy really have *feelings* for me all of a sudden?

"Why would you think that, Jimmy?" I replied. I decided to plow ahead and be strong. It seemed to be working on him these days. Besides, what was he going to do that he hadn't done before? "You're not supplying me the drugs you promised, and that's what I need, you *know* that. I'm an addict."

"But you were clean, for what, the whole time I was in?"

"Yes. I was."

"So, you can do it again!" He was *pleading* with me. What was this? "We could make a go of it Shannon!"

"What are you saying, Jimmy?" I asked, frowning.

He had a foreign look in his eyes that was almost...*sincere.*

"Listen, I don't want to hold you against your will anymore," he said, and I couldn't believe my ears. "It's no good. I want you to want to be with me. I stashed some money before I went to prison, a lot actually."

He fidgeted, rubbed his hands together, and then through his black hair.

"Shannon, we could go to Hawaii on our honeymoon, spend two weeks there, have a blast! You don't have to do drugs. You can just drink, okay?" He clapped his hands together, and then spread them apart, shrugging. "Whattaya say?"

The moron didn't realize he hadn't asked me to marry him yet; he'd skipped right to the honeymoon. As for my *wanting* to be his wife, I couldn't imagine it; but Hawaii? I had always, *always* wanted to go there!

A crazy thought popped into my brain: maybe he was changing; people did, by the way. Was it possible to make a marriage work with him? The way he had treated me, abused me? But maybe the combination of my quitting drugs again and his change of attitude would give us a chance, make a way for us.

Maybe marriage *itself* would change things for us. Plus, I *really* wanted to go to Hawaii.

"Are you asking me to marry you, Jimmy?"

He frowned and then shook his head, chuckling, and that was also a bizarre new twist - he *never* chuckled.

"I didn't? Oh, I went right to...well yeah, sorry. So, will you?"

I rolled the dice and answered in the affirmative. And two weeks later, after a trip to the courthouse to get hitched, we were Mr. and Mrs. Givazio on a flight to the Hawaiian Islands.

CHAPTER 24

Our honeymoon in Hawaii consisted of visits to three islands: Waikiki, Maui and Kawai. The beauty of the islands was breathtaking, more than I had imagined.

Jimmy had been congenial so far, a real prince, and I had lain off drugs, as promised. It wasn't so hard this time around, as I had not been as deep into them as long.

We reached the islands via cruise ships. Jimmy paid a fee of seven hundred dollars for unlimited food and drinks and all amenities on board. After setting sail, I ordered a drink at the bar and we went to our cabin to have sex. It was still just that for me, and I could not muster pretend pleasure every time. I think Jimmy sensed that, my lack of enthusiasm, but I was doing the best I could, all things considered.

At dinner we dined on succulent surf and turf, and I was thoroughly enjoying the cuisine and ambience. But Jimmy seemed distracted, not as chipper as he had been in New York.

"What's wrong, Jimmy?" I asked.

"Nothing," he grumbled. But there was. It was the first sign he was reverting back to his old self, and I should have seen it coming. But I was soaking up the moment, a dream come true trip to the Hawaiian Islands, and didn't give it much thought.

He finished his meal and excused himself.

"I'm going downstairs to play cards," he announced. There was a small casino area on the ship.

"Okay, have fun," I said, and he turned away without a peck or a wink.

Be that way, I thought. I had unlimited drinks at the bar, and I intended to find out what my limit was.

The bartender was mixing Mai Tai's, and we reveling passengers were knocking them back. He was good looking, and had been flirting with me most of the evening. It was his job, right? I was pretty loaded when Jimmy appeared behind me an hour or so later.

"How many of those have you had?" he asked. I looked back at him, frowning.

"What?"

"Is this your father?" the bartender asked me, nodding his head at Jimmy. I could almost hear Jimmy's teeth grinding together in rage. If looks could kill, the bartender would have disintegrated on the spot.

"I'm her husband, you jerk," he spat.

The bartender wisely found better things to do down the bar.

"I've got to go the ladies room," I said to Jimmy, excusing myself. I was too drunk to recognize just how angry he was, or hang onto that thought, or any thought, for long.

The restrooms were around a corner from the bar, tall plants placed at the entries. There was a short side railing off the bar and when I emerged from the little girl's room, Jimmy grabbed me by the hair and dragged me to that railing, slamming me up against it. There was no one else around. I could hear the ocean waves crashing as I looked into his bloodshot, rage filled eyes, and my heart sank. Here was the true Jimmy - angry, raging and abusive, and I knew I was in a world of trouble. His hand circled my neck, choking me.

"What did you do b***h?" he shouted, spittle flying off his lips, veins popping out on his neck. "Did you blow that bartender?"

I tried to protest, to tell him I had done no such thing, but he was cutting off my air supply, and I knew from past experience it would do no good anyway. He then drew back his fist and punched me harder than he'd ever hit me. Even in my drunken state I felt something come loose in my mouth, and I knew I was seriously injured. I was almost knocked unconscious by that punch, but he wasn't done.

He lifted me by the neck and waist, hoisting me up and over the rail. Suddenly I was falling, and I thought my days on earth were over when I splashed into the salty water of the sea and went under.

CHAPTER 25

Thankfully someone witnessed Jimmy tossing me overboard, and both security and crew moved quickly to detain him and fish me from the water. Considering the fact that I was drunk (although being thrown overboard and plummeting into the sea can sober one up a great deal) and almost knocked unconscious, it was a miracle I didn't drown before they got to me.

As they loaded me onto a stretcher, they assured me I would be okay, that they had the man in custody and he would be arrested when we reached the island.

"He's my husband," I croaked.

That apparently didn't mean anything to them, because when the ship pulled into port, I was taken to the hospital and he was taken to jail.

It took twenty-five stitches to sew up the inside of my mouth, and to this day my smile is distorted as a result of the damage caused by that punch.

The police took a statement from me (as best I could talk), and I was released with a prescription for Oxycodone, which I filled quickly. Not for the high this time. I was in serious pain, and needed the relief. Back at our fancy hotel room I popped a couple of pills, washed them down with an airplane bottle of Vodka, and fell back on the king size bed, contemplating the situation: Jimmy was in jail and there I was, with no money for a plane ticket to get back home. I had made a big mistake marrying him (understatement). I thought he had changed, but I knew now he never would, and would never stop abusing me. I wanted to leave him at that point so very badly, but I had no recourse.

The room phone rang and I answered.

"Shannon!" It was Jimmy.

"What do you want?" I mumbled. The pain medicine and alcohol were beginning to kick in.

"I want out of here! What do you think I want?" he whispered harshly. "Get my checkbook out of my bag and get your butt down here!"

I wanted to tell him he could rot in jail, but I really had no choice. I would bond him out, go along until we got back to the states, and then, hopefully, find some way to rectify my horrendous error.

The next two weeks were pure misery, despite the paradise around me. Jimmy apologized for hitting me and throwing me overboard, and that was sufficient, in his crazy mind, to end the matter and move on. We went ahead with our trip itinerary, and did the things married people do.

My dream trip had been thoroughly ruined, and I couldn't wait for it to be over.

PART II

Spiraling Down

CHAPTER 26

1990:

Back home in New York from our honeymoon, I immediately set about procuring drugs while Jimmy was gone to work. That fantasy of a changed life and happy marriage had gone up in smoke, and my mental state collapsed. I couldn't get high fast enough. I sought out Louie, mine and Trigger's old trick, and he was still above ground, ready and willing to strike up our old business deal. As soon as he got his, he gave me money and took me out riding to find mine.

About a month and a half later, I woke up a couple of mornings in a row, sick and throwing up. I had Jimmy take me to a drug store.

"What's up?"

"Just need some feminine stuff," I replied. I bought a pregnancy test, got a positive at home that night and sat on the toilet, staring at the plus sign in despair. I wanted to be pregnant, had for a long time; but not this way, not with Jimmy. I wanted to be clean and sober, have a family with a man I truly loved. But even though it was less than ideal circumstances, I was going to have the baby, no question about that.

"I'm pregnant," I announced.

"Really?" he replied, and I could see excitement in his eyes. "That's great!" He kissed me, and I cringed inside. "I've got to call dad, he exclaimed!"

They were happy for us and thrilled at the idea of being grandparents. They thought we were a normal couple, having no clue we met in a strip club, or that Jimmy had been a drug dealer.

I would like to say here that I stopped doing drugs, but that wasn't the case. I had gone back when we returned from our honeymoon, to escape the terrible mistake I made marrying Jimmy, and once you get back on that train it takes a lot to get off.

Jimmy had always imagined that one day I would love him (why he would, after all the abuse, I'll never know), that I'd clean up and we'd be one big, happy family. But he knew that was a fantasy, and so did I.

I did manage to get off the train three months before the baby was born, after my belly began to really swell. With that constant reminder of impending motherhood, I went into birth sober, and although I didn't get to feel that way long, I was proud of myself.

I delivered my first child, Tiffany, on July 15th 1990, a healthy baby girl, and that was a blessing considering the drugs I had ingested two thirds of the time.

I went home from the hospital with her, and even as I looked into her eyes with great love, I felt the itch, one only drugs can scratch. Jimmy's parents were coming around every day, and after the sixth day, my mother in law approached me.

"You look tired, dear," she said. "How about you take off for a couple of days? Go shopping, to a spa. She'll be fine here with us."

I seized on the idea. I could get high, scratch that itch, and come back to my baby. I just needed to get my thing on for a bit. I'd proven I could stop when I wanted to, having been sober for the past three months. I could do it, no big deal.

But I stayed gone for two weeks, going on a binge and losing track of time completely. I had quit and started back three times in the past two years, and, physiologically, my tolerance and need were increasing with each return. Nevertheless, it's very hard, if not impossible, to explain how a drug can have so much control over a mother as to tear her away from her child.

I could not get enough over that two-week period, snorting or smoking everything I could get my hands on.

When Jimmy's parents brought Tiffany back, and both he and I were gone, they went to court and filed a petition for temporary custody. Jimmy sent his goons to find me, and when they hauled me back, Tiffany was in absentia and Jimmy was in a rage.

"Look what you've done!" he shouted, as he slapped me around. "My stepmom and dad say we're unfit parents! What are you going to do now, you f*****g drug addict? We've got to go to court!"

I wanted to ask him where *he* had been, but I didn't dare. I took my beating, and the next day, I awoke with at least one clear thought: If anyone was going to get custody of my baby, it would be my mother.

CHAPTER 27

I had some breakfast and then took off for Louie's place to get my much-needed fix, and after our sex for drugs trade, I called my mom. This time I had stayed in touch with her over the past year, although I presented a prettier picture than life actually was. As far as she knew I was happily married and drug free, but she was about to hear the real story.

"Mom, I screwed up."

"What happened, Shannon?"

I told her the truth about my life and unhappiness: Jimmy beating me and throwing me overboard on our honeymoon, my return to drugs, and my recent two-week binge, resulting in the custody challenge by Jimmy's parents. As I told her the story of my inexcusable actions, being too stoned to remember to pick up my child, I felt like garbage. On the heels of that emotion I wanted to get super high and escape me, the woefully inept mother I was.

"I want you to have custody of Tiffany, Mom," I said, crying, and my tears were as real as my tortured soul was torn.

"When is the court date?" she asked, sighing.

"August 26th," I told her, sniffling. "And I want to go back to Tennessee with you and the baby! I don't want to stay here with Jimmy anymore!"

"I'll be there Shannon. But you have to get off the drugs, okay? You have to straighten up! You've done it before, you can do it again."

"Okay Mom," I agreed, but that agreement was worthless.

I rang off and went to Louie.

"I need a fix."

"You just *had* one."

"You want me to hang around?" I said seductively, stepping behind him and rubbing his shoulders.

"Of course I do."

I bent my head and whispered in his ear: "Then take me out and get me a *fix*."

I stayed with Louie leading up to the court date, and somehow eluded Jimmy and his goons. They didn't know about Louie's place, and when he took me out for my drugs, I made sure to move quickly and discreetly. I also made the old man cough up more money so I could buy in bulk and not have to run out all the time. I knew how to work ole Louie.

I was going through copious amounts of drugs by then, trying to numb myself and drown out that haunting voice whispering incessantly in my brain: "*You're a bad, bad mother you know that, don't you? Left your kid, got high and forgot about her, you did, you know you did, and you'll never...*"

"Shut up!" I would hiss aloud as I took a draw off the crack pipe, and then that soothing, euphoric high would come and silence the condemning voice.

Louie did my bidding without balking, because I was very good to him and he didn't want to lose me again.

As the hearing approached, Jimmy had no idea that my mother was going to attempt to take custody of Tiffany, and that I was planning to go back with her. I was wasted most of the time leading up to the court date, trying to kill the accusing voice in my head, and when the day arrived, Louie dropped me off a block away from the court house.

"Stay here. I'll be back in a little bit."

"Good luck," he offered.

At the beginning of the proceedings, I was almost too stoned to speak, rocking unsteadily on my feet, but I sobered up as time went on. Jimmy wore a smug expression throughout, confident his lawyer would prove me an unfit mother and he and his parents would be granted custody of Tiffany. When Jimmy's attorney was done making his case, the judge turned to me.

"Your Honor, I admit that I have issues, but so does Jimmy. I'm asking that my mother, who is here today, be given custody of my daughter."

"What? What's going on?" Jimmy exclaimed.

"Please contain yourself, Mr. Givazio," the judge warned, and then turned to my mother, asking her to state her name, relationship to me, etc. for the court.

My mother had hired a top shelf lawyer to represent her, and he proceeded to speak on her behalf, arguing her case for custody, mentioning her stable life, successful business etc.

It was enough. After my mother's attorney finished, the judge rather quickly granted custody to my mother, and Jimmy exploded, slapping the desk.

"Why don't you just cut my f*****g b***s off so I can't have any more kids!" he shouted, and the judge promptly charged him with contempt of court and had him hauled off to jail for a night's stay. That was alright with me - he would have probably taken a shot at me first chance he got.

Out in the hallway my mother hugged me and then held me at arm's length.

"Are you ready to go back with me and straighten up Shannon?" she asked. "You can be a good mother to your daughter."

"Yes Mom," I replied. "But I have to go get my things, pack, you know. I'll be back in a little bit." I was already itching for a fix, trying hard not to fidget in front of her.

"I'll take you," she offered.

"No! I mean, I've got a ride. He's waiting on me."

"You have to meet me back here at noon, Shannon, no later. We need to be leaving by 12:35PM.

It was 10:50 AM at that moment, and I shrugged. "No problem. It's not far and I don't have much to pack."

I went around the block and there sat Louie, patiently waiting on me.

"Did your mother get custody?" he asked.

"Yes!" I replied.

"That's great!"

He took me back to his place (after pulling over so I could score a rock) and I got my bag out, packing my clothes and toiletries.

After a few minutes, Louie appeared in the doorway of the bedroom I called mine when I stayed there. "You ready?"

I had finished packing, and he found me staring out the window at his garden, my arms folded tight against my chest. It was a nice kitchen garden, and I had watched him work it on several occasions. It seemed to me a peaceful, serene hobby, and I had wished more than once, while observing him, that I could find contentment in something like that.

"Yes. I'm ready," I replied.

But I wasn't, not even close.

We weren't a half mile from Louie's place when I asked him to pull over so I could score a hit.

"Just to take the edge off," I said. I bought a ten-dollar rock and smoked it behind a building close by. As I puffed and felt the moment of euphoria, I thought about what I was about to do: Go back to Tennessee with my mother and child and I would have to leave the drugs behind. Could I do that? It spoke volumes about my addiction that I would even ask that question of myself at that moment, but I told myself I could and I climbed back in the car with Louie.

"Let's go."

But a ten-dollar rock didn't last long for a hardened drug user like me.

"Stop," I demanded.

"You've only got fifteen minutes," he said. Old Louie didn't want me to go, but he understood, at the same time, that I was a mother now and I might regret it if I didn't make it.

"Just stop, I need *one* more," I sighed. He did, and I bought it and smoked it, leaning against a wall around the corner. I looked up at the clear blue sky - it was a cooler day in New York, a relief from the heat of summer, and as I began to float, I queried myself: Am I worthy to be a mother? Can I go clean, and stay that way? I can, I can, I can, I told myself resolutely, and got back in the vehicle with Louie.

"Now, I'm good," I told him. "Take me to the courthouse."

But the closer we got, the more nervous I became. My heightened anxiety was causing the calming effects of the drug to wear off more quickly than normal.

"One more time."

"It's too late Shannon. You won't make it," Louie advised, but I ignored him.

"Please, Louie," I begged, wringing my hands. "I can't do this without one more hit!"

He shook his head and looked over at me, sadness in his eyes. I didn't want to see that, so I looked out the window.

"If you miss her, don't you blame me, you hear?"

"I won't, promise!" I assured him.

I directed him to a corner where I got out, scored my rock and disappeared to smoke. This rock was *good* stuff. There are levels of quality in drugs, as anything, and this was top shelf. I puffed and sailed away, watching a bird flying high into the blue. I spotted a jet, leaving a contrail behind, and heard the old John Magee poem from a 70's commercial play in my mind: *Oh, I have slipped the surly bonds of earth, and danced the skies on laughter-silvered wings.*

I would miss my mother that day, I knew, and if I were honest with myself, I never intended to go. Deep in my heart I loved my child, but I knew she would be better off with my mother. She didn't need a tramp like me in her life, an irresponsible drug addict who cared only about getting high. That was the reality of my world then, what it was, no sugar coating it.

As a formality Louie drove to the courthouse, but she was long gone. I was an hour late.

Later that evening I called my mother and she ripped into me, telling me, "all you care about is drugs!" and she was right. I asked her to take care of Tiffany and softly hung up the phone, even as she continued her diatribe.

Now I had even more reason to hate myself, and the self-loathing would lead to increased drug use.

There would be no getting off this train for a long, long time.

CHAPTER 28

October, 1991:

"Listen, I've got a couple of things to talk to you about," Jimmy said as I sat across the table from him in our kitchen. He seemed terribly excited about whatever ideas were percolating in his brain.

A couple of his "associates" finally found me on the street, working. Louie had begun cutting back on my money, said things were getting tight, so in order to feed my drug habit I had to supplement by prostituting.

So, there I was back in Jimmy's apartment. He didn't beat me this time, just wanted to get down to talking about whatever was making him giddy and putting that sparkle in his eyes.

I had been emotionally broken for the past seven months, wondering about Tiffany, how she was doing. I called my mom to check on her, but she was terse and answered only the basic questions each time.

"Are you high?" she asked me once. "Don't call back here unless you're sober. You won't remember anything I tell you anyway." She hung up on me, and I cried my eyes out. There was never a time when I wasn't high - only more or less.

I stayed stoned all I could to escape the things I had done, but Tiffany's father had his drug of choice too: money. He didn't drink or do drugs, but he chased the almighty dollar night and day to feed his addiction.

"Okay, so here it is," he continued. "I've got a way for us to make a ton of money! And it's practically impossible to trace, if we move on every once in a while. So, we get these deceased people's social security numbers, driver's licenses, the whole works, their identities, right?"

"How?" I asked.

"Doesn't matter, just shut up and listen," said mannerly Jimmy. "So, when we get all this info, we open checking accounts under *their* names…"

"The dead people?"

"Yes! The dead people! Stop interrupting me! And then we write checks to buy stuff, and then return it to the store for cash!"

I understood what he was saying, but it sounded complicated.

"So how long does it take to set up?"

"Let me handle it, okay? Won't happen overnight, but you'll buy the stuff and return it, most of the time. That'll be your job, and you'll get a cut from every deal, okay?"

I would believe that when I saw it.

"So, what's your other thing?" I asked.

"Okay, here's the deal," he said, slouching back in his chair. "You're a working girl, right? My boys picked you up on the corner."

I looked at him, deadpan. "I do it for drug money, Jimmy. You know that."

"Alright, okay, doesn't matter," he said dismissively, waving a hand in the air. "Look, we're married on paper only, right? We know what it is between us - there ain't no love lost. But we can at least make some money behind this charade of a marriage, be business partners. What I'm saying is, if you're going to work, how about I set you up as an escort? You'll make more money and work less. And you'll have specific clientele that'll pay big bucks."

Sounded good to me. Who wouldn't take more money and less work?

"What kind of clientele?" I asked.

"Guys that like to be dominated," he said, "you know the type." I did indeed. "I even have a name for our escort business: *Carnation Domination*! So, what do you think?"

I laughed. The name was corny, but catchy.

"I don't care. You know what I'm after," I said.

"And you know what *I'm* after," he replied, his eyes twinkling.

CHAPTER 29

Jimmy bought the requisite blindfolds, handcuffs whips, etc., advertised *Carnation Domination*, and we went into business.

It was brisk right off the bat, and we soon had up to six clients per day paying hefty fees to be humiliated. As I plied my trade, Jimmy collected the money and gave me my cut, as agreed upon, money I used to buy drugs. He knew to keep me on a project he had to keep me high, and that was just what he did in the beginning, when it was in his best interest.

He worked out the details on the "dead business," and by January 1992 we worked our first deal.

"You ready?" he asked me in the store parking lot, and I turned my glazed eyes toward his from where I sat in the passenger seat. I had smoked up really good before leaving home. "You're freaking wasted!" he hissed. "Don't blow this! Tell me what you're going to do!"

"I'm going to buy a TV," I replied dully. "I know it's complicated, but don't worry about it."

"Right, why should I?"

I got out into the biting, cold January wind and made my way into the store, purchasing the television with a fraudulent check.

Three days later we returned it to the store and got a full refund, in cash. Worked like a charm. He had compiled a list of names and we methodically went through them all.

Between the escort business and the scam, we made a lot of money, enough to fulfill Jimmy's dream of moving to Florida.

And in mid-1993 we did just that, buying a house in Panama Beach. From there, we would ultimately begin an eighteen-month scam that would take us all over the country.

CHAPTER 30

It was quite a change of scenery and climate when we settled Panama Beach, Florida, from pines to palms and daily averages twenty-five degrees higher, which I appreciated given I had been cold most of the time in New York.

I loved the beach life, the warmth and sand, and that's what I enjoyed while Jimmy was busy putting together a huge list of names and records for our scam.

"This is going to make us so much money!" he exclaimed one evening as we sunbathed by the community pool. "I'm glad we're working together on this, Shannon."

I couldn't have cared less about his sentiment. All I wanted was my drugs, and I wasn't getting enough lately. I thought he would have the scam going sooner.

"When are we going to start? I need money."

"Well, you better get to work then," he replied. "I'm not there yet. Going to do it once and do it right. Make enough to retire on."

Retire? Who was he kidding? Not me. Jimmy would never stop chasing money.

I put in for a job at an upscale strip club (if there is such a thing) in Panama Beach, and the old birds tipped extremely well, enough that I could get and stay high.

That was my life for about six more weeks, until the day Jimmy told me I was done.

"We're going on the road. Time to make that cheese baby!"

I didn't want to leave Florida or my job, but I still had a healthy fear of Jimmy, so we packed our bags and took off.

CHAPTER 31

We visited all the major cities in the southeast, and upon arrival we would rent a hotel room and begin our shopping spree.

It took a few days to get the cash coming in on the returns, so in order to make money to buy drugs I would work the streets at night. There was an inherent danger in that; the established working girls in a given area jealously guarded their livelihood, and I was often persona non-grata in towns we visited. I would usually get in a couple of johns, enough money made to score drugs, before I was threatened with bodily harm. Most of the time, Jimmy would drive me around to buy. He knew that a high me was a compliant me, and he needed me as his partner in crime. I was subject to law enforcement stings occasionally. Jimmy would bond me out, and once collecting all the money from the fraudulent checks we would blow out of town, onto the next, leaving warrants behind.

My drug use was increasing, and I was putting myself in trouble's way in every city. I missed Florida, even New York, just somewhere I could stay in one place and live a low-key life, dance and do drugs.

About halfway through our scam journey we landed in Birmingham, Alabama and got a hotel room.

"I need a fix," I told Jimmy, as he sat at the cheap table near the window, going through his list. I was sitting on the bed, scratching my forearms and rubbing my dry eyes, my foot tapping nervously on the floor.

It was midday in the middle of summer, and the air conditioner was laboring mightily to beat back the sweltering delta heat and humidity. Jimmy's shirt was sweat stained in the armpits, but I had the chills, my teeth chattering. It had been too long since my last high.

He stood and sighed, his hands on his sides, and then he walked over, staring down at me balefully, shaking his head.

"You need a fix baby?" he cooed.

"Y...ye...yes," I stammered, and my teeth would not stop clacking together!

"Okay," he said soothingly, "But it's gonna cost ya."

"Wh...what? Any...anything."

And then he slapped me, full force, off the bed and onto the floor.

"That," he spat with disdain. He walked over to the door and opened it, then stopped and looked back at me. "What are you waiting for? Let's go!"

CHAPTER 32

"This town is tailor made for us," Jimmy said to me the next day. "I gotta get everything lined up."

After belting me, Jimmy had taken me out to get a fix, berating me the entire way.

"If I didn't need you to pull off these scams, I'd dump your sorry butt on the side of the road."

Now, as he worked at the table, I looked at him through narrowed eyes with pure, unadulterated hate. It was 9:00AM, and I was in need, not quite at the shakes stage, but I didn't want it to go that far. I didn't need him to take me to the area where the dealer was. There was one close by, as we'd discovered the evening before, but I *did* need the money, *my* money, to purchase my poison of choice, and I hated having to ask him for it. He held my share to secure my presence and participation in our (*his*) little operation. I wasn't going to get it any other way.

"Jimmy, I need some money."

"Why?" he asked, not looking up from his papers.

He knew why, he just had to make me say it. He never missed an opportunity to belittle me.

"You *know* why," I replied, "just give it to me please. Let's not make a big deal out of it, okay?"

He looked up at me with a wry grin. "It's a big deal to you, though, isn't it addict?"

I said nothing, just stared at him. Any further lip would earn me a wallop, if I hadn't already. He studied me for a moment and then rose, opening the briefcase and surprisingly tossing me a Benjamin.

"Go, get out of my hair," he said, and I wasted no time grabbing the hundred-dollar bill and exiting the room.

The hundred was enough to keep me out and about and away from Jimmy for most of the day, which was an absolute delight for me. I worked a couple of johns while I was at it, which made me flush with cash for a brief period. Of course, it didn't take me long to smoke it away, and in the course of wandering about the city I came upon a strip club. I entered the establishment; not very busy at 2:00PM, and I found the manager/owner at a table in the back.

"Hi."

He looked up at me, giving me a once over, and nodded his head. "Want to work?"

"Yes."

"Show me what you got."

I had to practically strip for him, but I didn't mind. I had become calloused in my conscience and jaded in my heart, going through the motions with total apathy. It was all about the drugs, no matter where I was or what I was doing. I filled him in on my experience at prior strip clubs while disrobing.

"Okay, can you start now?"

"Sure," I replied. "Where's the dressing room?"

He hollered at a stripper, and I followed her. I changed into an outfit I liked, made a pit stop in the lady's room to fire up my crack pipe, and went on stage for my first dance in Birmingham.

CHAPTER 33

Jimmy was cool with my working at the strip club while we were in town, anything to keep more money in his pocket. He drove me to work the next night, just to locate the place and keep tabs on me.

"I'll take a cab home," I told him when I climbed out of the van.

"Don't be out late," he warned. "We start buying tomorrow. I set up the accounts today."

Lovely, I thought. It was during the buying and returns that I had to spend the most time around Jimmy, and I hated every minute of it.

That night, as I danced and worked the pole, a man caught my eye. He was clean cut, handsome, and smiling at me. I worked my way over to him, and he generously tucked a twenty under my g string.

"Would you like some individual attention?" I asked, referring to the VIP rooms. They cost five hundred dollars, and a client there was treated to the natural privacy of the rooms, plus top shelf liquor and cigars.

"Yes, I would," he replied, smiling and displaying a perfect row of teeth.

I led him to one of the rooms, and asked for the fee.

He chuckled. "Oh, I don't have to pay, darlin'. I mean, I'll tip *you*, but...you're not from around here, are you?"

"No," I replied, looking at him quizzically.

"Well, see," and he leaned down, whispering in my ear, "I'm a police officer. Off duty at the moment."

"Oh! Well..."

"Still want to dance for me?" he asked. "It's good. I'm cool."

"Yes, I would *love* to dance for you."

As we mingled and talked I spun a tale of a bad marriage I had run away from, and how dancing was a temporary thing for me to make some money. He seemed to really like me, beyond that of a dancer for hire, and I reciprocated the feeling. For a moment in time, as I touched his face and looked into his eyes, I imagined we were lovers, and it was enough, that life needed no more than that to be complete.

When the dance ended, he surprised me by asking what I was doing after work.

"I had planned to go back to my room, but..."

"How about coming over to my place?" he suggested. "My name's Rodney, by the way."

"Shannon," I replied, giving him my real name instead of my stage name. "Sure, I guess that's okay. You seem nice."

"Oh, I am," he replied, laughing and smiling that winning smile.

He picked me up after my shift ended at 1:00AM, and took me back to his home in the suburbs of Birmingham. It was a nice place, and he treated me with respect throughout our stay together. Although it was pay to play, it seemed like more, and it was a taste of normalcy in the otherwise chaotic world where I existed. It was pure fantasy, though; Rodney was married, to a fellow police officer no less, and she worked third shift, allowing us our play time.

We fell asleep after our tryst, and the next thing I knew he was shaking me awake at 8:00AM.

"You've got to go!" I heard him say from my half-asleep state, but I popped fully awake a second later, two things slamming through my mind: Rodney's wife would be home soon and I was going to be late getting to Jimmy this morning!

He was going to be furious. Rodney drove me back to the club, paid me generously and peeled out.

"I'll see you soon, right?" he hollered.

"Yes!" I responded, waving.

His car disappeared and I stood there in the morning sun of Birmingham. It was already sweltering hot, and Jimmy was going to be even hotter. I did not want to return to Jimmy, especially after what I felt last night and the absolute certainty he would beat me as soon as he saw me. But he had my money, a lot of money, and that was the only thing that kept me going back. Even the allure of that was beginning to wear thin, however.

I would catch a cab back to the hotel, and walk right into the mouth of the cannon, but first I needed a fix... a *really* good one.

CHAPTER 34

Back at the hotel, Jimmy administered, and I took, my beating. I begged him not to punch me in the face, as it would hurt my business at the club to have a mangled appearance. He obliged (how *sweet* of him!), but doubled up on his slaps for good measure.

After that we went on our buying spree for the day, and I dutifully went from business to business, writing bad checks and presenting false I.D.'s. It was all so very criminal, but there is no code of ethics for an addict - all was done for the attainment and pleasure of $ and drugs.

When he dropped me off at the club that evening, he grabbed my arm as I went to get out of the car.

"We got another day of buying tomorrow. Come straight home after work, you hear me? Or else."

Later that evening Rodney dropped in, and we again went to the VIP room.

"Did you make it home in time?" I asked as I danced for him.

"Barely!" he exclaimed. "Man, it was close! We'll have to set an alarm next time. Like maybe tonight?"

"I can't tonight," I responded, although he had no idea how bad I wanted to be with him.

"Why not? I'm generous aren't I?"

"More than! I just have something I have to take care of, early in the morning."

I put him off successfully, and that night, as I left the club, I determined that I would leave Jimmy as soon as the scam in Birmingham was over. The money was one thing, and I wanted my part, sure; but I was tired of Jimmy's beatings, his constant disrespect and the overall lifestyle.

Over the next week we finished our purchasing and returns in Birmingham, and in between I went to work at the club, made good money and smoked it all up. Rodney and I got to know each other somewhat, and I spent the night with him again toward the end of our time there. He gave me his phone number, and told me to call him if I ever needed help.

"Are you going to take me to work?" I asked Jimmy one evening. "I'm going to be late already."

"You're done there," he replied, waving a hand in the air. He was lying on the couch watching some gangster movie on TV. I imagined he enjoyed the violent scenes immensely.

"Done? What do you mean?"

"I mean we're done here, in this town, and you're done working at the club! Got it?" He shook his head, annoyed. "We're heading out tomorrow."

"Well, give me some money so I can..."

"Go get your rock? You're pathetic, you know that? You can't go one evening without getting high...wait, where are you going?"

I was opening the door, heading out.

"Don't worry about it, okay Jimmy? I'm not going to beg you for money."

"Then go out and work for it, whore! Go ahead! Do what you do..."

But I slammed the door behind me, cutting him off. His butt was on the couch and wasn't getting up.

Outside the hotel, I looked up at the window to our room with complete disdain. With any luck, this would be good-bye and good riddance to that monster.

CHAPTER 35

It was 6:30PM when I exited the hotel, and I planned to call Rodney in a little while and see what I could make work with him. He was a policeman, and I thought he would be more apt to believe me when I told him I was Jimmy's prisoner, that the scam was all his idea and I had to go along with it for fear of my life (all truth). He could help me escape, but first things first - I had to work the street for some money to score my rock.

By 9:00PM I had made it with two johns, got paid well, and smoked up. Now it was time to call Rodney.

"Hey Rodney, it's Shannon."

"Hey baby, what's up? I'm sitting here in the club, looking for you."

"I couldn't make it tonight. Listen, can you give me a ride?"

"Where are you?"

I told him and he said he'd be along as soon as possible. I had moved on down to a better part of town, away from hooker alley, but I still found a spot around a corner and behind some bushes to hit my crack pipe one more time. Ten minutes later, he pulled up to a curb and found me sitting pretty on a bench. It was beginning to rain when I got into his car.

"Hello, Shannon," he said, smiling.

"Hello Rodney," I replied. He frowned briefly.

"Are you okay?" he asked, peering at my face, into my eyes. Could he tell I was high? And I was *very* high. I had hit that crack pipe hard, buttressing my courage to leave Jimmy, and now I looked wasted in front of Rodney, who had no clue I did drugs and it was probably best to keep it that way.

"Yes, I'm fine," I said, but I was sitting too rigidly, looking straight ahead to avoid eye contact with him.

"Alright," he said.

On the way to his place, I was too paranoid to talk much, and I silently cursed myself for over doing it. But that was the way of addicts, right? Everything could fall down, crumble to dust, it didn't matter as long as I got my drugs, my rock, my smoke. Addicts can't *think* beyond the next fix; consequences just don't matter.

I managed to make it into his house and up to the bedroom, with Rodney leading the way. I gripped the stairway railing as I climbed - the walls were swimming before my eyes, and I saw him look back at me concernedly. When I made it into the bedroom, I plopped down on the mattress, rolling over and looking up at him as seductively as I could manage.

"I'll be back in a few minutes, Shannon. Just relax."

He knows, I thought, *and he's not happy about it.*

I passed out, and awoke to Rodney shaking me.

"Get up! Get off my bed, you drug addict!" he shouted.

So, he did suspect me, but how did he know? I thought, and in the next instance, at the same time I looked down at my right sock where I kept my crack pipe and saw it was missing, my question was answered.

"Looking for this?" He waved the pipe in my face. "Take it and get out Shannon."

"Rodney, I..."

"I don't want to hear anything coming out of your mouth. I know your kind, I'm a police officer, remember? Just go, and don't ever come back."

I went out the door, on a long, arduous and sad walk back to hooker alley. Drugs had just ruined any credibility I had with Rodney, and now I was on my own, with no help to escape Jimmy and the torturous life I lived with him. But I was determined not to return to the hotel, to stay on course and somehow leave him behind.

CHAPTER 36

I made it to a homeless shelter, not far from hooker alley, and got a couple of hours of sleep before the sun rose. I had smoked the money I made from the two johns last evening, and now I would have to get to work early to earn my fix.

Jimmy had made all the money he was going to make in Birmingham, and I hoped I could elude him until he gave up looking for me and left. I couldn't go back to the strip club. He would be looking for me there, so I worked the streets, keeping a wary eye out for him.

After five days I took a cab out to the hotel where Jimmy and I had stayed, just a drive by check. Jimmy's car was gone, and I asked the driver to wait on me while I went in to the front desk to confirm he had checked out. I discovered he had, four days ago.

I felt shackles of fear falling away as I climbed back in the taxi. Could it be? Could it be that I was *finally* rid of Jimmy Givazio? I was certainly hoping so and felt it most likely. We (he) had made a lot of money to date, and he was probably tired of dealing with me. The feeling was mutual.

I was working the streets at night and staying at the shelter, but with my newfound freedom I began thinking about making plans to head back to Tennessee, closer to home, where I could visit Tiffany. The idea that I could see her on a regular basis was pie in the sky for now, but it was something to aim for someday.

Two nights later I was working a corner when a white van pulled up next to me, screeching to a halt. Out of the back poured three men wearing ski masks, who proceeded to grab me and roughly haul me into the back of the van. I screamed for help, but no one dared to approach.

I didn't know what was happening to me. The masked men tied my hands and feet, and I was lying on my side as the van pulled away. Then a window, separating the front seat and back of the van, opened and a face appeared. My heart sank.

"You thought I'd never find you, didn't you b****?" Jimmy said, laughing.

We arrived at a different hotel, but we were still in Birmingham. Jimmy had his goons take me to the room, and once there, he handcuffed me to a bedpost.

"You're not going anywhere this time."

He and the goons left, and I was alone in the bedroom for two hours, slumped on the floor. I had last smoked six hours ago, which was a long stretch of time normally, but after this I was badly in need of a fix. When he came back, he hit me in the head so hard it knocked me unconscious. At least I was out for a little while.

CHAPTER 37

I barely slept that night. After coming around from Jimmy's knockout punch I was beginning to suffer withdrawals, and by the next morning, I was chilling, shaking and scratching. From my place on the floor, still handcuffed to the bedpost (where I spent the night, while the chivalrous gentleman slept in the bed), I moaned.

"Shut up," Jimmy demanded, sitting up. "What's wrong with you?" he had the nerve to ask.

"Wha...what's wro...wrong with m...me?" I stammered. "I nee...need a fi...fix, Ji...Ji..."

"Stop, okay!" He swung his legs out of bed. "I need an espresso myself."

My eyes were itching and swelling shut, and I watched him pull on his pants and a tee shirt through slits. He looked down at me and shook his head in disgust.

"Guess I'd better go get you a rock before you die on me," he said. "I need you to make money for me, kiddo."

"Pl...ple...plea..."

"Can it."

It didn't take him long, thankfully. He was probably aware of the fact that I might *really* die on him. I smoked in the room, still handcuffed to the bed, and the relief was immediate.

"Now we're moving on to a different city," he announced.

Inside the car, he roughly handcuffed me to the door. "I'm taking no more chances with you."

A half hour later, he pulled into a truck stop to get some gas and snacks, leaving me in the van. Almost immediately after he put the cuff on I realized my wrist was too small for it. I had lost weight over the past couple of months, doing a lot of drugs and hardly eating, and when Jimmy disappeared into the store I wriggled my hand free with very little effort.

I got out of the van and took off running toward a rig that was climbing the exit ramp, hollering at the truck driver: "Help! I need a ride!" as I jumped up on the side step by the driver's door.

"What's wrong with you?" he yelled back.

"I'm running from my husband! He...LOOK OUT!"

Jimmy had come from nowhere, careening up the ramp and in front of the rig, driving the van right in front of the trucker and forcing him off the road. I leapt off clear of the rig before it went down the embankment, and no sooner had I rolled to a stop than Jimmy was there, grabbing me, pulling me to the van and into the back, and, using a length of rope, hog tying me. Breathing hard after his exertions (have a heart attack and die! I thought, but I could *never* be so lucky), he slammed the back doors and drove away.

I just could not get away from this man, but I would not give up. Someday, if he didn't kill me first, the right opportunity would come along.

Someday.

CHAPTER 38

January 1995:

By the time we finished our eighteen-month multi-state scam and returned to our house in Panama Beach, there had been a lot of money made. But I saw very little of my promised share, and after my attempted escape I saw no more. He took me to buy my drugs for the remainder of the trip, never letting me out of his sight.

We had been home for a week and he had not so much as mentioned the money. Now that the scam was over, I was fairly certain he didn't intend to ever give me my portion, but I had to ask.

"So, Jimmy, how about my share of the money?"

"Yeah? What about it?"

"I want it."

He laughed. "Are you kidding? You think I would give that much money to a drug addict, Shannon? That's the last thing you need. I'll hang onto it for you until you sober up. *If you ever do, that is.*"

He wasn't fooling me. He didn't give a hoot about my well-being. He would never give that money to me, whether I was high or sober, and I was through begging for it.

"I'm going to work," I announced. He was watching TV, another gangster movie, and didn't even grunt in response.

I went back to the strip club I had worked at before we went on the scam spree, and they rehired me on the spot. None of the girls I had formerly worked with were there, but it didn't take me long to find some fellow users and a supply line. I preferred stripping to prostitution any day - the dealers, and our clients, came to the club seeking us, rather than the far more dangerous reverse scenario.

I rarely saw Jimmy after going back to work. I danced into the morning, sleeping most of the day, and he was often gone when I awoke. I didn't know what he was up to, and I didn't care. I was still looking for my opportunity, the chance to leave him.

CHAPTER 39

After a month of dancing and flirting with various men that came into club, I was propositioned by a geriatric doctor in his early eighties.

He had sought me out and tipped me well for a week before his offering, and when he made it, I was struck by the similarities to Louie, although this gentleman, Oliver, appeared to be a few years older.

"It pains me to see you having to do this dear," he said. "If you'll come and stay with me, I'll see that you're taken care of. I'll pay you whatever you're making here, and then some."

It was an offer I couldn't refuse. I *did* like the ready availability of drugs at the club, but this was a chance to leave Jimmy, and that was the deciding factor. I could find the drugs I needed as long as I had the money.

I worked it out with Oliver to pick me up at the club the following evening, giving me time to finish the night's work and pack.

Jimmy was gone most evenings when I left for work, and this one was no different.

"I hope I never see you again," I whispered at the house as I slipped into the cab.

Oliver took me to his quaint home in a small town next to Panama City. He was impotent, so I didn't have to have sex with him, per se, but he did touch me. That was the extent of it, and it was a much better arrangement than any I'd had before.

The next two months, as spring made its way in, were fairly uneventful. I would drive his car to the bakery every morning for fresh bagels and I would, as part of the morning routine, see my dealer and buy my drugs. There was a spot by the bay where I would park and have my first smoke of the day, listening to the sea gulls and the sounds of the ships sailing through the harbor.

Since giving birth to her, I had always thought a lot about Tiffany, wondering how she was, but with special fondness in moments when I was alone. I made sure, no matter how strung out I was at different times over the years, to send her gifts on her birthday and Christmas; but it was always painful to sign the card from *Shannon*, instead of from *your mother*. She was going to grow up believing I was her sister. Of course, I had myself to blame for that, and when those negative thoughts came creeping in, I puffed harder and deeper on the pipe, trying to escape.

In those moments of reflection, my thoughts never turned to God, my eyes never looked toward Heaven. I did not hear a still, small voice calling me or a knock on my heart's door. But that's not to say there *was* no voice or steady knock - they were just inaudible to me, drowned out by the noise of the demons in my mind.

Someday I would hear the voice... and listen.

Someday I would hear the knock... and answer.

But not yet.

CHAPTER 40

I kept thinking that Jimmy and his goons would pop up on the street one day, maybe at the bagel shop or grocery store, and toss me in the van again, but it hadn't happened in the almost two months since I left. I still kept a keen eye out and looked over my shoulder, though.

I was lying out in the sun one day, by the pool behind the house, when Oliver approached me. "Hey, I bought you a lottery ticket."

I took it from him, shielding my eyes against the sun.

"Cool," I replied. It was a scratch off. "Got a dime?"

He dug in his shorts pocket until he found one and pulled it out, accidentally turning his pocket inside out and dumping the rest of his change on the concrete.

"Crap," he muttered, handing me the dime. "Here," he put the coin in my hand and bent down, grunting, to collect his runaway change. I helped him gather it up.

With that done, I began to scratch off my numbers. I didn't play the lottery regularly, and when I did, I never won anything so I wasn't expecting anything.

Except there *was* something this time -a *big* something.

"I can't believe it! Look at this Oliver! Am I seeing this right?"

He peered at the ticket and his eyes widened. "Why, you have won $10,000, Shannon!"

I squealed with delight, and my very first thought, which would be no surprise to any addict, was: *That'll buy a lot of drugs*!

But Oliver helped me think clearly about good use of the money.

"Why don't we go car shopping? You can get a nice one with this!"

It had been a long time since I had my own car, the first and last being the one my mother bought for me nine years earlier.

I found a brand new, beautiful green Camaro with a sunroof at a local car lot, and I fell in love with it on sight. The price was $13,500, a little above my winnings, but Oliver made up the difference.

"Happy Birthday and Merry Christmas," he said, hugging me.

"Thank you, Oliver!"

There are triggers for drug use, or increased use, but sometimes you just feel like doing more. That's what happened to me after I bought the Camaro, and, at the same time, Oliver cut my money in half, obviously reasoning that his contribution to my car was to be deducted from my allowance.

I wasn't happy about it, but I couldn't complain either. Oliver was good to me, and I'm sure he had no idea about my drug use, so I let it go.

The only problem was I still needed my drugs, what I was used to, plus a little more lately.

I couldn't go back to the strip club; same deal as the club in New York years ago: I had left with a client, no rehire.

So, I had to work the streets again, but this time with a twist.

I would do it out of my car.

CHAPTER 41

My car/prostitution scheme was safer than walking the streets and it worked out well for a month or so until one night, when I drove up to my usual corner to buy drugs from my usual dealer - but he wasn't there. In his place was another guy, and when he saw me stop at the curb, he sauntered over and leaned on my car door.

"Where's My Man?" I asked.

"Got busted," the new guy replied. "What you need, girl?"

There was a warning voice in my head, trying to tell me not to buy from someone I didn't know, but I was jonesing for a fix and deaf to the alarm.

"Rock," I replied, and took a twenty out of my purse. He slapped a cuff on my wrist as I handed him the money.

"Guess what?" he said smugly, "you're busted too."

I would say here that my heart sank, and I was scared, but by then I had been arrested over twenty times in my life. I knew the drill: I would be booked, charged, and bonded out in the morning. I had a pile of misdemeanors and warrants issued against me in several states, so this was nothing new.

On the way to the station, however, I realized I had a dilemma: Who would bond me out? I couldn't call Oliver. He was unaware of my drug use, and if he learned of it, I was sure he would refuse to help me. That left Jimmy, and I didn't even want to think about that.

At the station, they took my mug shot and led me to a room, where I was seated at the end of table. After what seemed like forever (my slow perception of time exacerbated by my need for the fix I didn't get) a tall, skinny black man, wearing a navy-blue suit and red tie, came into the room and took a seat about mid table. In his hand he had a folder, which he opened before him. It was my criminal record, no doubt.

"Mrs. Givazio, you have waived your right to an attorney, is that correct?" I had once requested, and gotten, a court appointed attorney, but that was early on in my criminal career, when I thought there was something to fight over.

"Yes," I affirmed.

"Mrs. Givazio is also correct, isn't it? You are still married to Jimmy Givazio?"

"Yes," I replied, no sense denying it, they had it all right there.

"So you were caught attempting to purchase an illegal substance from officer Pike," he said, as he looked over the report. I said nothing, as it was a statement, not a question. He looked at me with penetrating eyes. He was a very intimidating man.

"Mrs. Givazio, I have your rap sheet here. No surprise to you, I'm sure, that it's long and full of trouble for you." He let that hang in the air for a moment, and then reached inside his coat, producing his wallet and displaying his badge: FBI.

"I'm Agent Price," he said, "and I'm here to tell you that you're going to federal prison for a long, long time."

That got my attention.

"What? How long?" I had done time before, for thirty days, no big deal. But never prison. I didn't want to go away for a long stretch.

"Thirty years minimum," he stated. I stared at him, shocked. Was he telling the truth? He didn't blink.

"We have you and Jimmy on video, running your scam here in Florida," he informed me, "couple of purchases over the hundred-dollar limit. Now it's a federal crime. That plus your other felonies, and I'm thinking we can get them all bundled, so we're talking serious time here, Shannon."

"What can I do?" I blurted. The prospect of being locked up for that many years was too much to bear.

"Well, since you asked," Agent Price said, "there *is* something you can do." He leaned forward, his hands on his knees and looked sternly into my eyes. "I want everything. Tell me everything Jimmy has done, and we'll drop the charges against you here. But you'll have to answer the local."

I could live with that. He produced a recorder and I readily spilled the beans on all we had done.

When I finished, Agent Price cut off the recorder and stood. "Okay, very good Shannon. We could go after Jimmy right now, but we want our case as strong as we can get it. And we will get him, trust me. It's just a matter of time."

With that, he left the room, and I got my phone call. I hated calling Jimmy, but I had no choice. And who's to say that he would even help me? I had run away, been gone for three months now.

I might be stuck in a jail cell for a while.

CHAPTER 42

"Are you kidding me?" Jimmy exclaimed when I finally got him on the phone. "You leave me, and now you expect me to come and bond you out?"

"You wouldn't give me my share of the money you promised, Jimmy!" I whispered into the phone. "What was I supposed to do?"

There was a moment of silence as he digested this truth.

"Okay, so, I told you about that, the reason I couldn't give it to you, okay? But if I do this, get you out, you gotta help me, understand?"

"Yes, I understand," I agreed. "My car's impounded too."

"*Your* car? How'd you get a car?"

"I'll tell you about it, just come get me."

I drove back to our house in my Camaro, and when we arrived, Jimmy gave it another look over, whistling.

"Nice ride!" he exclaimed. "Come on now, how'd you get this? Did you steal it?"

"Nope. Won the lottery. $10,000."

"Really? I don't believe it!"

"Believe what you want," I said, already sick of him. "It's mine."

I didn't tell Jimmy about the FBI. Why? Because I wanted him arrested, gone, out of my life, then I could get a divorce and move on at last.

It turned out that he wanted me to go with him on another scam spree, into Texas again for starters. So, after he beat me for leaving him (it was standard operating procedure for Jimmy) he would say, "You know I gotta do this, babe" before he began wailing away), we packed up the van and took off.

CHAPTER 43

We were on the road for eight months, working the scam back through the states, and while it was no fun being around Jimmy, I knew there was an end coming, a day when we returned home and the FBI would arrest him and send him away for a long time.

Excited by the prospect of being free of Jimmy at last, I was on my best behavior for the duration of the trip. Consequently, Jimmy kept me in drugs, and actually gave me a portion of my share of the money.

When he had scammed all he could get away with, he drove back to Florida.

"Well, we did pretty good Shannon," he said as he pulled into our driveway and killed the engine. He looked over at me. "You were a good helper this time around."

I shrugged. "Just doing my part."

He got out of the vehicle and was taken down by federal agents and police officers pouring out of unmarked cars, vans and, apparently, dropping from the sky.

"On the ground Givazio!" It was Agent Price. He had a gun to the back of Jimmy's head and was cuffing him with the other hand, a well-practiced move. "We've got you now! You're going up the river for a long time!" He was laughing about it. Jimmy was not.

I stayed in my seat, watching as they pulled Jimmy roughly to his feet, read him his rights, and stuffed him in the back of an unmarked car to be whisked away to places unknown.

It was May 1, 1996. I had met that vile man when I was just eighteen years old. I was now twenty-six, and had been around him for most of those nine years, suffering tremendous physical and verbal abuses. My smile would forever be altered and a finger rendered useless because of him. I breathed a heavy sigh of relief as the car drove away, and I saw him looking back, straining his neck to see me.

I would never lay eyes on him again.

CHAPTER 44

With Jimmy gone, I drove to Oliver's place to see if my old benefactor might forgive my leaving him as I did, and perhaps be open to restarting our prior arrangement. But instead of the old man, a middle-aged lady answered the door.

"Is Oliver here?" I asked.

"Well, *you* must be Shannon," she replied truculently, her nose in the air. "My father is no longer living here. He's in assisted living. You won't be able to steal money from him any longer."

"Now wait a minute, I didn't steal anything. I..." but she closed the door in my face.

I went back to my car and climbed in behind the wheel, shaking my head. Poor Oliver! He didn't need to be in a retirement home! Sure, he was old, but he was still able to get around, and his mind was good. His kids just wanted his money. *They* were the thieves! I had at least earned the money he gave me. They just stuck him out of sight and mind.

That day I looked around and realized everything in Florida I had been there for, by choice or not, was gone. I had a daughter in Tennessee I had not seen in a long time. I wasn't clear of drugs at all, but I would have to convince Mom of that, at least for one evening, in order to see her. Chattanooga was only thirty minutes away from Mom's house, and I could work the streets there, make enough money to score drugs and occasionally get to see my daughter.

With that determination, I got on I75 North and began the nine-hour trip back to my home state.

CHAPTER 45

I rolled across the Tennessee state line out of drugs and needing a fix badly, so I exited I-24 onto fourth avenue, toward the projects, where Trigger and I had been years before on that terrible night when we were raped; but it was also drug central, and I remembered (although my raddled brain might forget a lot of other things) where to find the drugs I needed.

Standing on a corner littered with empty beer cans was a black man, and I pulled up, rolling my window down.

"Yo," he hailed. "Watchu want?"

"Rock," I replied, waving my money at him.

"Here ya go." He handed over the merchandise. "Hey, where you gonna smoke up?"

"Somewhere around here."

"You want to hang with me? I got a place."

I was a drug addict, jonesing so bad I had no thought of where I was or what I was doing. I just needed to get high. Besides, I had no real concern for myself anymore. I had been through hell and I really didn't care what happened to me.

"Sure," I replied.

He got into the passenger seat and introduced himself.

"Henry Lee," he stated.

"I'm Shannon."

He directed me to a sparsely decorated duplex/crack house. I lit up on the sofa, and he sat next to me, smoking a blunt and looking me over.

"You a workin' girl?"

"Yeah," I affirmed, feeling the wonderful high. "I've done it all, dance, the street, you name it."

"Where you going from here?"

"I just got in town. I'm going to visit my mom."

"Well, you look me up when you're done, okay? I got a lot of girls working for me. I treat 'em right."

I bought another rock or two for the road and left Henry Lee with his drugs and girls for the night. It was 8:30 PM, and I would be pulling into my mom's driveway in thirty minutes.

CHAPTER 46

"Shannon!" my mother squealed when she answered the door and saw me standing on her stoop. She hugged my neck and pulled me into her house.

"Hi, Mom," I responded, hugging her tightly.

No matter the things one does, or the coldness in one's heart for the world at large, your mother is the only one you've got. I wept in her arms, for the times before, the innocence of childhood, all the things we went through together. Holding her, I remembered *me*, a time when I wasn't an addict just looking to get high every waking minute of my life. It was brief, but it was there; a time before Mr. Holland, when I wasn't on the run, trying to escape my past, or chasing the attentions of men, trying to find the affectionate father I never had.

She pulled back and held me at arm's length. "Look at you Shannon! My god you're so skinny! When is the last time you ate?"

"I don't know."

She led me to the kitchen and tried to feed me what was left over from their dinner. I picked at the food, unable to do much with it. The stimulant class of drugs is a major appetite suppressant, hence the reason I was so thin.

"Shannon, you've got to get off the drugs and eat," my mom urged. "Please go back to rehab! It worked for you before, remember?"

I did remember, but I wasn't ready to do that, not by a long shot.

"Where's Tiffany?"

"She's in bed, Shannon! Its 9:15PM."

"Well, can I see her? I won't wake her."

"Sure, honey."

As I stood beside her bed, staring at my five-year-old daughter's lovely, angelic face, my heart swelled with unspeakable love and immeasurable regret. I wept softly, the tears flowing down my cheeks, for the times with her I had missed - her first steps, her first words.

I knew beyond doubt she had been better off with my mother than with an irresponsible drug addict like me over the past five years, and that truth, that drugs had a greater hold on me than even my child, tried and condemned me as I stood there.

"I love you my baby girl," I whispered, bending and kissing her lightly on the forehead.

My mother and step dad were standing in the doorway when I turned around and rushed past them, sobbing and covering my mouth. I ran down the hallway and out the front door, and my mother caught up with me as I got behind the wheel of my car and started the engine.

"Shannon, please don't go!" she begged, but her words fell on deaf ears. I *had* to go and get stoned out of my mind. I could not be sober with my current thoughts and live; it was that simple. "Where are you going? Please tell me so I'll know where you are!"

"Chattanooga, Mom," I told her. "I'm not leaving Tennessee."

I drove off before she could say more, to the streets of the city, where, with a lighter, rock and pipe, I could kill my negative thoughts.

CHAPTER 47

I parked my car on the side of the road along a nocturnally busy street, frequented by johns looking for hookers and hookers looking for johns. I plied my trade for four hours, making enough money to score my drugs and rent a room at Craig's Lodge, a cheap motel known for renting to prostitutes and drug dealers.

The rooms were less than desirable, to say the least, but after my evening at Mom's place, and the psychological aftermath, I just wanted a place to smoke, get high and pass out, which I did in short order.

I awoke to the sounds of housekeeping banging on my door. I rolled over and looked at the surprisingly operational digital clock by the bed: 10:00AM. I had slept for a while, and it felt good.

"Go away!" I yelled.

The maid was Hispanic, and, through the door, she let loose a flurry of words I didn't understand, although I am positive she was cursing me in her native tongue. I heard her knocking on the next door down, wait for and receive no response, and then open the door with her key and gain entry. I hoped it made her happy to have something to clean.

I spent the day getting and staying high, and that night, I parked my car on the side of the road, ready to work.

The very first john I made an offer to was an undercover cop. They were running a sting and I, along with every hooker on the street, was arrested and taken downtown. My car was impounded, and as it is with a prostitution charge, I would serve a mandatory three weeks before being released - no drugs, nothing to help me escape my miserable mind.

CHAPTER 48

Those three weeks, without drugs to help me through the minefield of my thoughts, were perilous times for me. I would work, with the rest of the girls, picking up trash along the sides of the highways during the day: bottles, cans, cigarette packs, etc. At night, we were confined to our cells, and the first couple of nights were spent, if one was an addict like me, suffering withdrawals. I would say that was the worst of the time spent there, but it was actually the easiest for me. In my physical suffering, I was distracted from my mental anguish; but when I was clear of the withdrawal symptoms, the real pain kicked in - the pain of sobriety, and the voices that tormented me without end.

Why weren't you there for her, Shannon? Why couldn't you quit the drugs and be a mother to your baby? Why? Because you're a DRUG ADDICT, that's why! A useless, good for nothing DRUG ADDICT who no one will ever want, that the world would be better off without! Love will NEVER find you again, don't you know that? Your daughter won't miss you...she doesn't even KNOW you! So go ahead, end it, no more suffering, no more pain, no more sorrow, no more rain...

And if there had been means by which to do it, I would surely have ended my life on a couple of occasions in that stretch. I had no God to turn to back then but *my* god, the almighty crack pipe, and I would serve him wholeheartedly as soon as I was released.

One of the bright spots of my incarceration at that time was meeting Annette - a tall hour glass figured red head with a pretty face and a strong disposition.

"That was some sting, huh?" she remarked one day as we were cleaning up the roadways, early in our confinement. "More cops than I've ever seen involved in that one!"

"Yeah, it was crazy," I agreed, glancing at her, and she smiled at me pleasantly. Then, out of nowhere, a stocky black girl sidled up to me, poking a finger in my chest.

"You wuz workin' my space," she growled.

Annette was suddenly beside me, towering over her by a good eight inches. I hadn't realized how tall she was until then.

"You better back off, sister," she growled back, "if you want to keep that finger." I was shocked she had come to my defense, and I was immediately grateful.

"I see how it is," the girl said, looking at Annette and me. "You two be love birds, huh?"

"Maybe we are," Annette replied, taking a step forward, backing the girl up. "What's it to you?"

The girl had nothing else to say, so she simply grumbled something under her breath and moved on. Annette looked at me and flashed that beautiful smile. "I don't swing that way, honey, just for the record."

"Me either," I replied, laughing. "Thank you."

Annette was always kind to me, and I had found a friend for life in a sometimes rough and ugly world - but she could be a terror to anyone that dared cross her.

After I did my time, it was a desperate woman that made it to Henry Lee's place, begging for a crack rock and a pipe to smoke it with. Ole Henry Lee hooked me right up, but with a caveat.

"You have to promise you'll be one of my girls now, and I'll take good care of you, okay?"

With him dangling that crack pipe and rock in front of my hungry eyes, I swore on everything in existence that I would be the best girl Henry Lee ever had, bar none.

"Okay, here ya go Fruit Lucy," he said (a street nickname that stuck, and one most of the girls, dealers and even cops knew me by), handing the paraphernalia over. I had brought Annette along with me, and she also joined Henry Lee's stable.

We lit and smoked together and I sailed away at last, achieving the mind-numbing effect I so desired, except I noticed something – those voices didn't *entirely* go away this time. Sure, they were barely there, just whispers, almost inaudible, but still *there*.

It's just because I went without too long, I thought. *The more I smoke, the less I'll hear. That's the ticket.*

And I kept telling myself that: over, and over, and over.

CHAPTER 49

My car was impounded, so when Henry Lee offered to let me stay at his place, I accepted. He took the rent and the cost of the drugs I used out of my earnings, so I never saw the money after I handed it over to him, which was all good with me. As long as I got the drugs to knock out my thoughts and a place to lay my head, everything was as good as it could get.

"Good stuff here," Henry Lee opined as we sat on the sofa at his place one night, any night, they all blend together when you're high.

"Yeah it is," I agreed, puffing the pipe as I sat beside him, my feet up on the rickety coffee table. "Are you getting it from a new supplier?"

"Yep," he replied. "Got a better..." BOOM!

"What the...?" Henry sat up, and I froze, eyes wide.

The crack house was a duplex, and whatever was happening was going down next door, where another dope dealer lived. We heard a breaking sound, the door coming down, and shots rang out. It all happened quickly, and then a bullet came through the wall, whizzing by us, hitting a lamp and we hit the floor, spread eagle.

"Stay down!" Henry Lee shouted, and more bullets began coming through the wall, thudding and imbedding into the sofa, splintering a chair and shattering a beer bottle.

We stayed quiet as mice after the shooting stopped, not wanting to draw any attention to ourselves. Henry Lee crawled to an electrical strip and killed power to the remaining lamp and TV.

We laid there motionless, and it was a hot night, sticky and humid. I suddenly felt the need to pee.

"I need to pee," I whispered to Henry Lee.

"Okay, I think it's all clear," he said, beginning to rise. "We've got to get out of here before..."

And then the sirens blared and the cops were pulling up outside, shining lights all over the building.

"Get down!" Henry Lee hissed. He dropped like a brick and pulled me down to the floor with him. "Don't move, don't make a sound!"

"But, I've got to..."

"Shut your mouth Lucy!"

After a couple of minutes, we heard a rap on our door.

"Anybody in there?" an officer bellowed. "Hello?"

We said nothing then, or later when the detective and coroner showed up, all through the investigation that night. I had to release my bladder and I went on myself, no choice. After a few minutes it became uncomfortable.

"I've got to change my clothes," I whispered to Henry.

"What? Lay still! You gonna get us caught Lucy!"

"I peed on myself Henry. I'm going to crawl to the bedroom and change."

"Alright, but don't get us found out!" he whispered harshly.

I began snaking my way across the floor, inching forward. My hair was wringing wet, and sweat dripped from my forehead into my eyes. The heat was so oppressive I thought I was going to die from a heat stroke. I thought Henry would before I did.

I changed clothes and stayed put, rolling onto my back, exhausted. At some point I fell asleep, and when I awoke the next day, Henry Lee greeted me as I staggered into the kitchen.

"Come on lazy bones! Time to get out there and make Daddy some money!"

Good ole Henry Lee.

After surviving that terrible night, life got back to normal on the streets, as normal as life can be there anyway. Henry Lee controlled three blocks of prime real estate for his girls, and I took full advantage, working all the johns I could to keep my situation.

I didn't realize the impact seeing Tiffany would have on me. I had been using drugs and alcohol since I was twelve years old to escape the things that happened to me and, later, the things I had done. But nothing was harder to live with than the knowledge that I was the mother of a five-year-old child who was growing up with the false belief that I was her sister.

One night I was working my corner and a john pulled up, rolling down his window, all normal - but when I approached, I saw the face of my step dad.

"Hey Shannon," he greeted, smiling.

"Hey Dad," I replied, duly surprised. I had talked to my mother from jail, and told her I was working in this area, but I didn't expect my step dad to come looking for me. "What are *you* doing here? This is a rough part of town."

"I know. I could ask you the same thing, right? How about getting in, taking a ride with me. I won't make you do anything you don't want to do. Promise."

And I knew he wouldn't lie to me. Gordon was a good husband to my mother and an honest, integral man.

"Okay, just for a bit," I agreed.

"How about something to eat?" he asked after I got in. I suppose I looked terribly thin to him, and I was. I hadn't been consuming my RDA in calories in a while, but lately I had almost abandoned food.

"I'm not hungry," I replied.

"Look, Shannon, you *have* to eat. At least try, okay?"

"Okay."

He drove to a local burger joint and we went in and found a table. The steamed, square sliders sat before me, the smell of meat and onions and bun wafting into my nostrils. I could remember a time, years ago, when those iconic little burgers were appealing to me and I had eaten them with gusto, but now I was fighting off a wave of nausea. Gordon ate one with an eye on me. I had to make an attempt, so I took a bite and chewed slowly, my head down.

"Shannon, you know how worried we are about you, especially your mother. She can hardly sleep."

I chewed and took a sip of soda to moisten my dry mouth, one of the side effects of heavy drug use.

"She wants you to come home and go back into rehab. You know it's the right thing to do."

I shook my head.

"Why?" he asked. "It worked before, it can work again. This life is no life at all. You're not going anywhere Shannon!"

I slumped back in my chair, staring at him. I was high, of course, and incapable of making sound decisions in that state, which was how I liked it. My only concern was when I was going to get my next fix.

"Take me back to the corner," I requested.

"You've hardly eaten a thing."

"I'll take it with me, if that's okay."

He sighed. "I told you I wouldn't make you do anything you didn't want to do, and I meant it. You have to *want* to do a thing for it to work."

He took me back to where he found me and let me out. There wasn't a whole lot of conversation on the way - what was there to talk about, other than the obvious?

"Take care of yourself, Shannon," he said as I climbed out of the car. "I'll be back to see you again soon, okay?"

"Okay." I had nothing to say to that. "Bye, Dad."

He drove off, back home to my mom and Tiffany, and I quickly resumed my trade. However, the fact that, he, would risk his life searching for me in a bad neighborhood, for God knows how long until he found me, that meant more to me than that man, or anyone, would ever know. And I would remember that moment for the rest of my life!

CHAPTER 50

Over the next two months, Gordon came to see me every other weekend. I would get in his car, we'd go somewhere for food that I would hardly touch, and he would inform me how worried mom was, that she was praying and begging for me to come home.

I wanted to get higher and higher, that was my goal, and getting the amount of drugs I needed to do that was no problem. I was a real trooper, raking in the dough for Henry Lee and he, in turn, was tossing those rocks my way.

Still, something was happening inside of me during that time. All those visits with my step dad were having an effect, as I thought more and more about that period in my life when I went to rehab and got sober. Before my renewed dreams were dashed, and that ugly video was made, I had been hopeful about life and love; but that had been before Tiffany was born, before my dismal failure as a mother.

How could I ever feel that hopeful again? One thing I knew from experience, however - although drugs could temporarily help one to escape painful thoughts and problems, they could not create hope in one's heart. Absent the perfect love of God, which covers one's *entire* existence in grace, drugs were the only thing I had to escape my past. But one can *never* find any future with them, no aspirations and no new chances.

I had been mulling these things over, taking longer breaks in between fixes, just to see how it felt, if I could maybe do it again, and when Gordon showed up the next Saturday night I climbed in his car and said: "Take me to Mom. Go *now.*"

He looked at me with a shocked expression, and then a huge smile spread across his face. "Really?"

"Yes," I replied, and I broke down and wept, sobbing on his shoulder as he drove me back to my hometown.

CHAPTER 51

The first couple of days at Mom's I stayed in bed, sweating, shivering and shaking. When I was coherent, she brought me chicken noodle soup and cheese sandwiches. I could manage only sips and nibbles at first, but after four days I was gobbling food down, my starving, famished body demanding sustenance.

My mom had been talking about my going back to rehab from the beginning, as I floated in and out of consciousness. By the time I was over the withdrawals, I was ready to commit. I knew if I wanted to get back to a normal life, where love and reconciliation and being in Tiffany's life were possible, I had to try.

"I'll go," I told my mom, and she flung herself on me, hugging my neck so hard I thought she was going to break it.

The next thirty days in rehab were spent in meditation, group therapy, crafts and chanting, the standard things like *The Prayer of Serenity* and "It works if you work it!" stuff like that. I knew from my first stint in rehab that the real struggle came when you left those facilities, back into the real world, and that would be my, and everyone else's, challenge when our time was up.

The condemning voices were not silent in my head during rehab, but they were less frequent, and my depression was lifting. When I arrived back at Mom's house, I was greeted at the door with hugs and smiles, and Tiffany was holding and hiding behind my mom's leg, wary of me. It hurt my heart to see that, her fear and lack of recognition, but I hid my disappointment and smiled.

"Hi, it's good to see you!" I said.

"Say hi to your sister," Mom instructed her, and... bang! Another shot to the heart. It was innocent enough on my mom's part. She had raised Tiffany as her own for six years, and referred to me as Tiffany's sister many times over that period, I'm sure. Still, it hurt like the devil, and I straightened as Tiffany slid further behind the protective leg of her known mother.

"It's okay," I said, tears forming in my eyes, but before the faucet could turn on full blast, I suggested: "Let's get some ice cream!"

"I have some in the freezer! We can make milkshakes," my mom said. Tiffany clapped her hands, delighted by the idea.

Later that evening, after Tiffany was put to bed, I sat with my mom and dad in the kitchen, talking about my rehab time and sobriety.

"I do feel better," I said, and that was true, "and I want to keep going with this. My sobriety, I mean." And I *did*, and I *didn't*, and every addict knows what I mean by *that*. "I would like to get a job, something to keep me busy."

They both shook their heads vigorously in agreement with that statement.

"But I'll need reliable transportation...my car...it's impounded." I played with one strand of my braided hair as they looked at me in silence for a moment.

"Shannon, I'm afraid you'll just take that car and go right back to Chattanooga and..."

"No I won't Mom," I replied confidently. "Look, I went to rehab, I'm trying to do things to stay clean. You've got to trust me for it to work. I have to have a car to get a job."

"She's right about that," Gordon chimed in, backing me up, and thank you Dad! And let me say here that I didn't want my car back with the intention of returning to drugs or the lifestyle I had led. She really *could* trust me this go around. I felt better than I had in a long time, and I wanted to make sobriety work for me, to find love again, to one day, maybe, be able to tell my daughter who I *really* was.

I did want my car back, however, because I *loved* my green Camaro! It was mine, bought and paid for, and I wanted to drive it and show it off every opportunity I got.

"Okay," my mom agreed, and I jumped from my seat, hugging them both, thrilled.

CHAPTER 52

Once I got my car back, I didn't really go looking for a job all that hard. Mom gave me an allowance for lunch and gas, just enough money to ensure I wasn't buying drugs. Not that it was a problem for me, not then. I was clean, and but for that nagging feeling that is part of life for an addict, no matter what stage of quit they're in, I was good as I could be. I had to balance the time I spent around Tiffany and my mom together, though. Pretending I was her sister was a hard pill to swallow, and sometimes I felt I would choke on it.

It was late summer of 1996 when I met who would be the father of my second child. I had been clean and sober for two months, and I was out cruising around in my car - my favorite thing to do, minus drugs - in a neighboring township. It was a rainy evening, a bit cooler than it had been. Summer was running out of steam as fall whispered its impending arrival.

I saw a guy, walking on the side of the road, and even in inclement conditions I could tell he was handsome. The rain was coming down harder, and I pulled over and rolled down the window.

"Hey, get in!" I yelled, and he did, without hesitation.

"Thanks!" he said, running a hand through his wet hair, and looking at him I hoped, in that moment, that something might come from this, that this handsome guy would maybe love me and I would love him. Then I would have another chance at a normal life, and I would cling to it, hold it with all of my might as my bad days drifted further in the past, fading to just a blip and finally out of sight. He looked at me as I stared at him, and laughed. "I'm Jackson."

"Shannon," I replied, smiling and averting my eyes for a moment.

"Nice ride. New?"

"Yes."

"Well, take me for a spin!"

"Okay."

We drove around for a little while, and traded stories about high school and life after that. I left out all the bad stuff about me, but told him I had lived in Florida and New York, and was married but separated, that my husband was in prison.

He told me he was unemployed at the time, and I gathered he'd had a sketchy work history from the information he provided. But it didn't matter to me then. I was blinded by my desperation to make something work, so much that when he suggested we get some pot, I agreed.

"I know where to get some," I bragged.

"You do? Cool! I don't have much money, though, right now, being out of work and all."

"Don't worry about it, I've got it."

I went to the projects near my hometown, where I had bought drugs years ago, and found, as always in the world of commerce, the players change but the game doesn't. I had enough allowance money to score a dime bag, and we went to a secluded area to smoke it.

I rolled the joint with a practiced hand, and he was impressed.

"Done that a few times, huh?"

I shrugged and handed the finished cigarette to him. He lit up and puffed, passing it to me, but I refused.

"Come on baby," he coaxed, flashing a smile.

And just like that my two months of sobriety - all in the name of wanting to keep his interest in me going, for the dream of knowing love again - went up in a toke. I savored the inhalation, holding it to get the maximum hit. I was a pro at it.

"There ya go," he said, smiling in his high and looking at me appreciatively. I knew what that look meant, and I was a pro at that too. After my experiences in life, one would think I would recognize how misguided and wrong it was to begin a relationship on those notes - using drugs and having sex. But my need to be affirmed and approved by a man that loved me ruled my thoughts and emotions, as it had for years, and I could not see the error of my ways.

Later that evening, I dropped him off at his place, a shabby mobile home he shared with a friend.

"Hey, come by tomorrow evening, let's do it again," he said, leaning in my car and kissing me softly on the lips. I looked into his eyes and felt a fluttering in my heart.

"Okay," I murmured. He slapped the roof of my car and jogged inside.

As I drove home I noted the hour was late enough that my mother would be asleep by now, so I wouldn't have to deal with attempting to cover up my drug use. I told myself that I would not venture into harder drugs than pot this time, that I was only doing it to ingratiate myself to Jackson, and that was the truth.

In that moment.

CHAPTER 53

In the beginning, as with Josh many years before, Jackson expressed interest in me, treating me with respect even as we had sex almost every night. It was the first time in years that I was sleeping with a man for reasons other than money, drugs or fear, and it felt so good, so right in my irrational heart and mind. In the first month we would smoke pot or drink, have sex, then cuddle and talk afterward as he whispered sweet nothings in my ear.

I was steadily falling in love with him, my blinders firmly affixed, unable to see that he was using me. He didn't have a job and wasn't looking for one, content to mooch off of me as long as I would let him.

I began to come around to the realization that he wasn't in love with me by our third month together, and by the end of that month I was sure of it. We went to a bar at the foot of Lookout Mountain, just outside of Chattanooga, on the weekends, and one-night Jackson got drunk (as he would want to do) and began telling some of his drinking buddies that I had fake boobs and permanent eyeliner (both true, bought and paid for by my husband). It was demeaning and disrespectful that he would share, in a sneering tone, personal information I had divulged in confidence to him.

I felt betrayed and foolish, that I had given so much for nothing, that my dream of love, someone that really cared about me and wanted me, was over and gone again. I was no more to him than one of the many johns I had sex with as a prostitute.

I'd had enough. I ran out the door of the club, straight to my car, and Jackson ran out behind me.

"Shannon! Wait!" he hollered.

"No, Jackson!" I shouted in response as he came down from the deck toward me.

"Where are you going?"

"Away from you! You don't love me!" I cried, and the tears were coming now.

"That's not true!" he protested, and only because I was his meal ticket and he knew it was disappearing.

"Yes it is! I'm not stupid, Jackson. I just wanted a relationship, someone to love me the way I loved them!"

"But I do lo..."

"Don't!" I interrupted him. "Don't say it! Don't lie to me anymore! Just leave me alone." And I got in my car, slamming the door, starting it up and stomping the pedal. The engine roared as I peeled out of the parking lot.

What was I thinking? That I could come back home, sober up and somehow become a respectable citizen? After all I had done, all I had been through? I couldn't change what I was any more than a leopard could change its spots. I realized then that no one would ever love me or want me in the normal world. The only place I could feel I belonged was on the streets, where I could get high and escape and no one would judge me.

As I approached the on ramps to I-24, west to go back home to Mom's place, or east to Chattanooga, the choice for me now wasn't even close. Pot wouldn't do it anymore, I needed something stronger, something that would again take the pain of betrayal and lost love away.

With tears in my eyes I took I-24 east, back to Chattanooga and the crack pipe, a life I knew so well.

CHAPTER 54

I went straight to Henry Lee's place. He wasn't there, but Annette was, getting ready to go out, and she gave me a big hug.

"Shannon, darling, I missed you!" She practically lifted me off the ground.

"I missed you too," I replied, and I genuinely did. Annette was a good friend to me.

"Henry's out selling, but he'll be excited to see you! What are you doing back here anyway? I thought you were gone to rehab, got all clean."

"Oh, I did, but it didn't work out for me. Listen, you got a pipe and a rock?"

"Course I do, sugar. You sure?"

"Yes, I am."

She produced the items and I lit up, feeling the euphoric rush, the high that would take me away again. I felt some guilt, after all the effort (money) on my mom's part to get me clean, but it was nothing a few more tokes on the pipe wouldn't take care of, and I proceeded to do just that.

I returned to my previous position as Henry Lee's number one girl. He took good care of me, and Annette and I took care of each other.

About a week later I was working the street and a john pulled up to the curb, waving me over. I approached his window and felt my stomach churn and my heart gallop in my chest. It was none other than Tony, the guy who raped me and took my virginity that awful night over thirteen years ago.

The self-absorbed psychopath didn't recognize me, apparently, so I got in the car with him and directed him to Craig's Lodge. I took his $100, and then seductively undressed him, all the way down to his birthday suit. As he lay back on the bed, anticipating my strip dance, I stopped and stared hard at him.

"Did you used to live in Glenville, and come up to the roller rink on the weekends?" I asked him.

"Yeah. Yeah, I did. That was a long time ago. Why?" he asked, frowning.

"Because I'm the girl you took behind the steam plant and raped, you son of a b***h!" I hissed. "I'm taking your hundred dollars!"

His eyes widened, but I was out the door and gone. No amount of money could ever make up for what he did to me, but at least I took something of his, I surmised, and that's the best I could do.

CHAPTER 55

It had been a few weeks since I left Mom's house, making my decision to return to the world of drugs and prostitution, and as I said before, every time I quit and went back, it seemed my tolerance for the drugs increased after a while. By the time the cold days of December rolled around, I was in the grips of the crack pipe to a greater degree than ever before. It wasn't hard to get there either - I was living with Henry Lee, along with Annette, and he kept us well supplied with rocks.

Naturally, for a working girl, the warmer months are much preferred to the cold, damp days of fall and winter. You have to wear more clothes, cover up the merchandise, but not *too* much. There was a dress code, per Henry Lee you see, so I tended to desire a higher state for that reason as well - it was easier to deal with the frigid temperatures.

One morning I awoke very sick, just making it to the restroom in time to throw up what little food I had in me. I sat on the floor by the toilet, the nausea hitting me in waves, and then Annette was beside me, her arm around my shoulder.

"We need to get you to the Health Department and get a pregnancy test," she advised.

"What?"

"Just do it, okay honey?"

It was a crisp, cool day, the sun shining brilliantly from a deep blue sky when we exited Henry Lee's place around 1:00PM. As Annette drove, I looked at the Christmas decorations displayed in retailer's windows, at all the normal people, sober and clear eyed, walking down the streets, into the shops, without need of mood-altering substances, and I envied them. I wanted to be one of those people, seemingly able to seize the day and cope with life as it came, revel in the happy moments.

But my need to escape, my need for drugs, was greater, as had been evidenced now by two failed rehabs. As far as I could see, my chances of becoming one of those normal, happy people were slim to none.

I had to leave my thoughts in the car, as we had arrived at the Health Department to determine my condition.

There wasn't a great deal of care and concern for my kind there. They saw it all the time - drug addicted mothers who had no business getting pregnant. And the test confirmed I was indeed.

"You have an option here, Mrs. Givazio. You are not too far along to consider having an abortion..."

I held my hand up. "Just stop right there, okay? I'm *not* going to have an abortion," I said forcefully. Although I wasn't ever going to win a mother of the year award, I did not believe in abortion, not then, not now. All life is precious and meant to be, and none can be replaced, and I believed that with all of my heart even then (despite my behavior).

The nurse sighed and continued her speech in monotone, (which I tuned out) and gave me pamphlets explaining what to expect when you're, you know, with child, bun in the oven, etc. I had been here before, and I knew what to expect. I tossed the literature in the trash on the way to the car.

"Girl, what are you going to do?" Annette asked when we got in the car. "Do you know who the father is?"

"Yep, I'm pretty sure I do," I replied.

CHAPTER 56

That evening, I drove back to my hometown, to the trailer park where Jackson lived, to let him know he was going to be a father. On the way, I entertained fanciful thoughts – fueled by my crack pipe - that upon learning of his new status he would be proud and take responsibility, desire to change his ways, get a job (if he hadn't acquired one) and settle down with me and our baby. That was a life I could quit drugs for, a second chance at motherhood, to do right by this child. I could make it happen, but I needed Jackson to step up, and there was a chance he would.

I was full of hopeful expectations as I knocked on his door, but when he opened it, my heart sank a bit. There was a half-naked girl on his couch.

"What are *you* doing here?" he rudely greeted me.

"Can I talk to you?" I asked, glancing over his shoulder at the girl. She was smoking a joint.

"What about?"

"Just come outside for a minute," I requested, walking down the shaky, slapped together wooden steps. He followed me reluctantly, and I leaned back against my car. He stood in front of me, arms folded defiantly.

"So, what gives?" he asked impatiently. "I got company, in case you didn't notice."

"Yeah, I noticed. Listen, Jackson...I'm pregnant."

He shrugged. "So? Why are you telling me?"

"Because it's *your* baby!" I exclaimed.

He shook his head vehemently. "Oh no. No, it's not. It's somebody else's."

"I'm eleven weeks pregnant, Jackson! It was you and me! *You're* the father!"

He laughed. "Yeah, right. I don't know what you're trying to pull, Shannon, but it ain't gonna work. You ain't pinning that on me."

Unbelievable! I stared at him, speechless for a moment, and then found my voice.

"You don't have a job yet, do you?" I asked softly. "That girl in there, I bet she has one, and I bet she's buying your food and beer and pot, isn't she?"

He laughed at me, shaking his head. "I'm done here. If that's all you came here for, so are you."

"You're a loser, Jackson," I said as I climbed back in my car, and I don't know if he heard me or not, but I was about to cry and I couldn't let him see me do that.

That so didn't go right, I thought as I drove away, tears streaming down my cheeks. *The odds are just stacked against me, everywhere I turn. What am I going to do? I have to stop the drugs, earlier this time, for the baby's health, and I will, after just one more hit, one more night. I need that.*

Just one more.

CHAPTER 57

March, 1997:

It's all good, it's all alright, it's nothing and it's everything. Nonsensical thoughts born of a nonsensical action as I steered my Camaro with my knee while lighting my crack pipe.

I was high as the sky and going higher, like a helium balloon on the 4th of July, needing to get stoned while driving, because that was fun to do - get high and drive, I mean.

I had returned a week ago from a sixty-day stint in an Atlanta correctional facility, compliments of a years old outstanding warrant in that city for drug possession and prostitution, and I was smoking crack, one more time, that same lie I'd been telling myself for the past two and half months--just one more, just one, but I couldn't hold to it, not so far, but I'd been clean for sixty days while I was in the pen! That counted for something, right?

So, I deserved this, one more for the road, so to speak, especially considering what I had to do to get my car out of impound. I had to call a trick to come pick me up and bring me back to Chattanooga, and pay my car out. For that, he got all the sex he wanted. This, after all that, was my reward, and I was doing a good job driving with my knee while lighting my pipe, and was it catching?

Then a loud smack, a crunching sound, and I felt a bone rattling jerk. I'd hit something or someone hit me, I was in a blender, going round and round and then...

Gone. Nothing but blackness.

"Can you hear me? Miss, can you hear me?" a voice asked a second or a minute or five minutes later, I don't know.

"I'm pregnant," I said, and blacked out again.

CHAPTER 58

I was taken to the hospital, and both the baby and I checked out fine. I was relieved by that knowledge, but as soon as I was released, I caught a ride with Henry Lee back to his place.

"Your car was totaled, Fruit Lucy," he informed me, and *that* was heartbreaking. My green Camaro, gone!

Annette gave me a gentle hug when I arrived at the pad.

"Baby's okay, huh?" she said, softly patting my belly.

"Yes, all good."

I had a night in the hospital to think about my actions, what I was doing to my body with the drugs and lifestyle, and I knew I should quit now like I did before with Tiffany, the last trimester at least. But it seemed easier to quit back then, when I was younger. Now the drugs seemed more ingrained in my life, in my body chemistry, and staying with a drug dealer didn't help.

Not long after I settled in, I got a rock and a pipe from Henry and fired up, thinking again: *this will soon end; I will stop for the baby.*

Of course, I didn't, no matter my good intentions. The drugs had a death grip on me, and even being with child wasn't enough to break it this time.

CHAPTER 59

A week after my brief hospital stay Henry Lee was arrested during a major drug bust. I found out from Annette when I came in off the street.

"Shannon, they took him away!" she cried. "What are we going to do?"

"We've got to get him out," I said, "find out how much his bond is."

"Yeah, my bond's high, Lucy," he told me the next day when I visited him. "They want to keep me in here."

"I'll get you out, Henry!" I exclaimed. "I'll get the money!"

"Don't worry about it," he said. "That's a lot of money, Lucy. They got me."

I left, resolved to raise the funds to get him out, no matter his insistence that I give up. I needed him back on the scene. I had worked hard to be his number one girl and that status provided me with a lot of perks, namely lower priced drugs, much lower than the street price, and protection. Henry Lee was respected on the street, and so, by virtue of my association with him, was I. I had a vested interest in his return.

So I worked a lot over the next month to make and save enough, and I would have had it sooner except for the dual issues of my drugs costing more from other dealers, and my habit not diminishing in the least.

While Henry Lee was locked up, his regular customers would come by and we had to direct them to other dealers, while reassuring them he would be back in business soon. There was a brother and sister that came by about once a month, and they finally showed up for their party favors.

"Hey, how are y'all doing?" I asked.

"Good, just here for some stuff," the guy said. "Where's Henry?"

"He's in jail right now," I informed them.

"Oh no!" the sister exclaimed. "So where do we go?"

"Well, I know a dealer. I can tell you how to get there."

"We don't know much about this part of town," sister said. "Could you show us?"

These two were harmless, and you wouldn't suspect they even did drugs from looking at or talking to them.

"Sure," I responded. "Wait here a minute, okay?"

Anytime I left Henry's place, I took the money I had saved up for his bond (almost enough now to get him out) with me, because those thieving girls, save Annette, would steal it first chance they got. I retrieved the money from under my bed, and returning, I climbed in the backseat of their nice, newer model car.

The brother was driving. "So where to?"

"Just go left here," I instructed, and soon we arrived at the dealer's corner. I was impressed with them. They seemed like regular people, company I rarely got to keep, so I pulled out some of my money and bought all around.

"You don't have to do that," the brother said, "we've got it."

"I want you to know me and Henry appreciate you!" I exclaimed, shoving the money into the dealer's hand. I wanted them to like me, and when the brother, after pulling away from the corner, next asked me to go to their house and get high with them, I was thrilled.

"Sounds like fun!" I said.

Their home was in a nicer neighborhood, and their mother greeted us when they opened the door.

"Well, who's your friend?" the middle-aged version of her daughter said.

"This is Lucy, Mom, she's going to hang out with us for a little while," the brother let her know, and we went upstairs to his bedroom.

After lighting up our pipes and getting our high on, the sister leaned in with an inquisitive look.

"So are you a..." she began.

"Prostitute, yes." She giggled, and so did I.

"What's that like?"

"Not so bad, you know, I mean sometimes you get a beater, but it comes with the territory. Henry Lee takes *good* care of me."

"So he's your pimp, right?" the brother remarked. "And he's in the can. How long?"

"Not much longer!" I exclaimed, puffing the pipe and feeling the high. "I've been working hard and raising money!"

"For what? A lawyer?" the brother asked.

"No! His bond. I got to get him out!" "So how much do you have to pay?"

"Five hundred dollars! I've got four-fifty now, almost there!"

"Wow, cool! You keep that money in the bank, I bet, right?"

"No!" I replied, laughing, and I reached inside my bra, pulling out the roll of cash. "It's right here! I don't trust banks or ho's!"

They laughed with me, and I was enjoying the shared experience with these two. They were gainfully employed (as they informed me on the way to the house), and were obviously not junkies. For a period of time I felt normal, like we were all friends, part of the fabric of society sitting around after a week's work and doing our weekend thing.

The hour was late, and the brother stood. He didn't seem as high as, say, *I* was, nor, it appeared, was his sister. "Let's get something to eat, I'm starving!"

I was rarely hungry, but I thought I could eat right about then. The relaxed atmosphere of the evening had sparked my appetite.

But what happened next was one of the most surprising moments of my life.

CHAPTER 60

Brother and sister and I were just merrily riding along to somewhere to eat something when brother pulled over into an alley way.

"What's up?" I inquired, my head on a swivel as I was tripping along, and suddenly brother was out of the car, opening the back door and roughly pulling me outside.

"What?" I sputtered, my shocked, uncomprehending mind trying to grasp what was going on, and then sister - now the parallel universe "evil" version - appeared beside me, swinging a beer bottle at my head with all of her might, growling even. The blow knocked me semi-unconscious, staggering me, but I was still on my feet, and this apparently enraged evil sister so she hit me again and that did it...I went out.

When I awoke in the alley way, the duo was gone, and I immediately checked my bra for the money - also gone.

My heart sank. All my work, all that money saved to bond out Henry Lee, stolen by two who I would least suspect would do such a thing.

Although I was distraught over the money, I had to turn my attention to my body (which had not yet fully recovered from the auto accident). From the ache in my ribs, they had added a couple of gratuitous blows while I was out. I struggled to my feet and thumbed a ride to the hospital emergency room to get myself, and the baby, checked out.

Upon release, I thumbed again until I made it back to Henry's place. Annette awoke when I entered.

"Hey...my god, what happened to you?" she exclaimed, seeing the knot on my forehead.

"Beaten and robbed," I replied. "They stole the money."

"Oh Shannon, forget the money, did you go to the hospital? How's the baby?"

"Yes. Baby's fine, I'm fine."

She sighed and put a comforting arm around me. Annette showed the world a "don't mess with me" tough persona and brave face, but behind that fierce exterior she had a tender, compassionate heart that very few were aware of.

"Thanks Annette, you're so good to me."

"That's what friends are for," she replied, smiling.

CHAPTER 61

A month later, still chasing the rock, I had another dead-on look at the worst of human nature. It was, perhaps, the most horrific thing I've seen or been involved in, and it started with meeting a couple, much like the brother and sister who beat and robbed me. They were regular customers, showing up every Saturday to buy from Henry Lee, but this time the boyfriend had an idea, and he invited me into his car to discuss it with him and his girlfriend.

"So, I've found this supplier, willing to sell in bulk for a low, low price," he informed me. His girlfriend was riding high and very animated.

"Yeah, yeah, yeah!" she exclaimed, "like half price, you know, BOGO!"

"Buy one get one," the boyfriend explained, and I didn't bother to tell him I knew the acronym.

"Is it for real?" I asked. I wanted it to be. I was paying almost twice as much for my drugs since Henry Lee went to jail.

"Yeah," he replied. "Ten-dollar rocks for five. You just have to have the money. We got half of it, so we wanted to let you in on the deal. Split it, you know?"

"How much?"

"Two hundred."

"Let's go," I said, without giving it another thought.

I didn't know the couple well. I had seen them buying before, said hi, that was about it. The girlfriend and I sat in the back lighting up while he drove.

"This is going to be so great!" she squealed, and when her sleeve fell back while firing her bowl, I saw track marks on the inside of her arms. Heroin addict too. Shooting up had never been my thing, but who was I to judge anyone? That was a hoot!

"Almost there," the boyfriend announced from the front, and soon pulled up to a curb I recognized. It was a little off the beaten path, but I had walked it before.

"Alright, show me the money," he said, turning around in his seat and facing me.

"I'll come with you," I said, reluctant to hand that much money over to him.

"No, it's better I go in alone, in case things get hairy," he advised. "I'm not going to make off with your money! My girl will stay here with you!"

I considered it for a moment, then reached into my bra and paid out two hundred dollars to him.

"Sit tight! Be right back!" he said, climbing out of the car.

"Here you go," the girlfriend said, pushing the pipe in my face.

He wasn't gone long, and he jerked the door open in a rush, getting behind the wheel and peeling out quickly.

"Did you get the stuff?" I asked.

"Yeah," he replied, out of breath and nervously checking the rearview mirror.

"What's wrong?" I asked.

"Nothing, okay?" But he was very agitated. "I got it all. We'll divide it up back at my apartment."

His place was a couple of miles from the dealer's residence, a little on the outskirts of the mean streets, but close enough, as the songs says, for rock n' roll.

He came to an abrupt stop, the jolt causing the girlfriend to drop the pipe.

"Hey!" she said angrily. "Look what you made me do!"

But he was out of the car and running toward the house before I could get my hand on the door handle. I watched him, the bulging coat flapping out as he ran, and just as I wondered what he was running for I heard a car's tires squeal and several shots - rat-a-tat-tat - and saw him go down.

My head seemed to turn in slow motion toward the car from which the gunshots emanated, but it was already pulling away further down the street.

"Oh my God," I whispered, and then the girlfriend was scrambling out of the car, running toward his motionless body. I followed, looking around as I went, making sure the shooters weren't coming back.

"Where are they? Where are the drugs?" his girlfriend hissed, digging in his coat. "Come on, help me, the cops 'ell be here in no time!"

I stared at the horrific scene before me with incredulity. The boyfriend was most likely dead and his girlfriend had no regard for his life, her sole concern at the moment securing the drugs before the police arrived. It was a truly frightening experience to witness the hold substances could have on a person, and I couldn't bear to see it any longer.

I would surmise later that he somehow stoe/ made off with the drugs *and* the money, but at that point, I didn't care about any of it.

"Where are you going? Don't you want your part?" I heard her saying behind me.

I covered my ears and ran.

July, 1997:

Henry Lee wound up being released on time served and came back to his place as our pimp and the established dealer in the community. I was almost full term and still having that "one more" fix, I am so ashamed to say, but it's the truth about so many pregnant women who are addicts. The drug *owns* you, and you can't imagine going through a day without that *feeling* that keeps you going.

I called my mom to talk about the baby as I approached my delivery date, and she was quick to state, in no uncertain terms, that she would *not* take on another child, period.

That I still had a living baby in my womb was a miracle in itself, given the prodigious amount of drugs I had consumed over the course of the pregnancy, but life wants to happen as God ordered it.

One day, in the sweltering heat of July, my water broke and I went to the hospital, where I gave birth to Allison (I had not bothered to learn the gender of my baby during my pregnancy, but if it were another girl, I had decided to name her Allison, despite the fact I would be giving her up) on July 27th 1997. She was born premature, weighed 5 lbs., and was drug addicted; but otherwise she was a healthy baby with no other complications.

I made the painful call to Bethany Christian Services to come and take my baby from me. I was an addict, and profoundly aware of my ineptitude as a mother in my condition. And even if I wanted to take my baby with me, the law required, because she was born addicted, that I go into treatment and be under regular supervision after. And if I managed to do that, where would we go? Back to a crack house? I had no address of residence, no way to provide care for a baby, and it just wasn't feasible.

Knowing Allison would be *much* better off with a stable family did not lessen the pain of surrendering my child to a stranger. Even through the cloud of addiction, and the logic of my decision to give up my baby for adoption, the maternal instinct groaned within me.

Gloria, the lady from the agency, arrived as I held Allison in my arms, staring into her sweet face.

"Are you sure you want to do this?" she asked, and is there a harder question to answer in the affirmative in the universe? *Hey Mom, Mother, Mama,* a voice spoke up, unbidden, in my mind, *you just gave birth to a baby that's been inside you for eight months, give or take, and here she is, ready to suckle, see her reaching, puckering, wanting mother's milk? And now you're going to hand her off to a stranger and let them take her away from you forever? You okay with that? Is that cool?*

"Yes, I am," I whispered, tears rolling down my cheeks, and Gloria reached for her, but I held on for a moment, not wanting to let go, not wanting to surrender my baby. But finally I did, a whimper and sigh escaping my lips.

"I'll be back with some papers for you to sign tomorrow, dear," she said gently, and as she went out the door with my baby in her arms the moment felt surreal. Did that just happen?

If I ever needed to escape from something, it was that last scene in my life, and I would have gladly taken a long toke on my crack pipe right then.

Living with my thoughts was not going to get any easier from there.

CHAPTER 62

Gloria came back the next day with papers to sign and fill out. She told me there would be a court date to make the adoption official.

"What is your address?" she asked me. I was sitting up in bed, scratching my arms, fidgeting. I was going through withdrawals, and barely able to focus on what she was saying. I was scheduled to be released soon, and it couldn't happen soon enough for me.

"I d...don't have an address," I told her. "We all j...just live together at this place. But you can take my mom's address, that's the l...last place I got mail."

She took that down, and upon my release from the hospital she gave me a ride back to Henry Lee's place. On the way, I begged her for money to buy food and cigarettes (but, you know, I *really* wanted to buy drugs with it, as fast as possible).

"Can't give you money, dear, but I'll buy you some food," she said sweetly. I *was* sort of hungry, so I took her up on that. But as soon as she dropped me off, I hit the street, looking for work. I didn't even bother going in to see Henry Lee. He would just send me back out to make money. So there I was, just had a baby, still bleeding, and out on the street to do all I could do: perform oral sex on johns, to get enough money to buy a fix and boy did I need it bad by then!

After a couple of encounters I had enough to score a rock from Henry, so I went back to his place and we smoked our pipes together sitting on a tattered sofa.

"So, Fruit Lucy, you had that baby, huh?" he remarked.

"Yes," I replied, drawing heavily, wanting to kill my thoughts, those voices that had started up in my head again.

"So where's it at?"

"I don't want to talk about it, Henry," I said, and the finality in my tone made him shoot me a look. But instead of challenging me, he simply shook his head and resumed working on his pipe.

I lit and drew to smoke away the awful thing I did, and when that high wore off, I went out and worked to buy more, to smoke more, ever more, trying in vain to cover the sins of my past, and a part of me just wanted to die, to end it all.

What I didn't know then was that my sins could not only be covered, they could be washed away, erased forever - and that not only would I die, but I *must* die spiritually, and only then would I be...

...born again.

PART III

Finding My Father

CHAPTER 63

The year following the birth and adoption of my second child was the last one of my twenties, and I went into a downward spiral worse than at any time before in my life. I was spending the nights working the streets, hooking, and doing drugs back at Henry's place, day in and day out. I was skin and bones, hardly eating, and I got arrested several times for prostitution. The police who worked that beat knew me well, and one evening, just after I had purchased two crack rocks, a cop car pulled up alongside me as I sashayed coolly along.

"Hey, where're you goin, Fruit Lucy?" he hollered. I recognized him - he was a skinny one who had arrested me a couple of times before.

"Just going to the store!"

"Come on, I know what you're doing!"

He braked and got out, and I quickly popped the two rocks into my mouth.

"You holding anything, girl?" he asked. "Up against the car, you know the drill."

I did. It wasn't my first rodeo. I spread, hands on the roof, and he frisked me, finding my crack pipe and a single rock in my pocket. I had totally forgotten about that one.

"Okay, this is enough to take you in Lucy. Never going to learn are you?"

I had to get rid of the rocks in my mouth. I saw my chance as he opened the door, and I spit them in the grass on the other side of the walkway.

He cuffed me, not very tightly I noticed, and put me in the back of the cruiser.

"Let's take a ride downtown," he said.

"Okay," I responded, as though I had a choice in the matter. But my mind was working feverishly on a plan of escape. I had to get to those rocks; if I didn't, and soon, someone else would find them and take them and I couldn't have that, couldn't dare let that happen.

I was in the grip of paranoia and obsession at that stage in my life, the crack pipe and drugs all consuming, altering my perception of reality. There was a time, not that long ago it seemed, when I would awake to the day and be okay for a bit before I smoked, but not now. Now, I had a rock at the ready, and almost as soon as I opened my eyes I lit up and stayed high until I my head hit the pillow at night, if I even went to sleep.

"... gotta try sometime," the officer said, something I didn't catch.

These handcuffs are loose enough, I bet I can slide right out of them, I thought. And if I can do that, I can slide that metal door open between the front and back, get up there and kick this skinny copper in the head! I could do it too. I had gotten tough over the years, in and out of jail, living on the streets. I had once been a weak sister, afraid to fight, bullied by those girls in high school, but boy they wouldn't want to face me now!

Anyway, if I could get to him, I could distract him enough to get him to pull over and I could escape out the front passenger side door. Had my plan; now to execute.

It went perfectly.

He pulled off onto the shoulder, braking and tires screeching as I bit his arm and nose and pummeled him about the face.

"Ow!" he screamed, a bit girly, and I would've said something about that but I was busy opening the passenger door and sprinting across the median.

It was cool that my plan had actually worked, but I was one worn out girl by then. A year and a half of heavy drug use, extreme most recently, and malnutrition, had left me emaciated and weak. I was good for the fight to escape, but the fleeing part was not in me. My legs simply gave out and I collapsed, falling to the ground.

It seemed I had only been down for a few seconds, but suddenly I was surrounded by policemen who had answered the officer's call for back up. I tried to get up and run again, but they tackled and hog tied me, feet and hands cuffed together, and I screamed like a madwoman as they carried me to the side of the road. I was dehydrated and delirious and things were fuzzy around the edges, the world going in and out of my field of vision.

"I need to go the hospital," I muttered, and they concurred, calling an ambulance to take me.

After I was rehydrated and released from the hospital, an officer took me to jail. It was no big deal to me by then. I would stay overnight, bond out in the morning and go on about my life.

But this time would be different. I had so many failed payments that I couldn't get anyone to bond me, and I was stuck in jail with pending court dates on eight misdemeanors and six felonies, very serious stuff I would now have to answer for.

Henry Lee had not come to visit me, and I didn't expect him to. He couldn't show his face around law enforcement. My mom wouldn't take a collect call from me, and I didn't blame her. I had given her nothing to believe in for a long time now.

After a few days of sweating out the drugs and going through withdrawals, I found myself sitting in my cell, reflecting on my life as I faced grim prospects.

I had come to the end of the line, it appeared. I knew the charges against me would lead to prison time, and I was extremely worried about that. Although I had been to jail for brief stints throughout my life, it wasn't the same as the big house.

I thought about my father, or lack thereof. Who knew where he was now? Probably getting drunk or high somewhere, a selfish man who never demonstrated love for me or provided an example for how a man or father should conduct himself. I thought about the only true love I had known, early in my life - in a sea of wrong, Kevin and I had been something right, and I had ruined that opportunity. How I tried getting married, tried stripping, even a lesbian relationship in jail once. Not even my children could impact me to the point of effecting real change in my heart and lifestyle.

What had I *not* tried?

God.

I had never tried God, given Him a chance. There were chapel services in the jailhouse where I was incarcerated. As I closed my eyes to go to sleep, I decided to attend one of those next Sunday, give it a shot.

What did I have to lose?

CHAPTER 64

I went to the chapel for Sunday services with my mind wide open, ready to listen and learn all I could about the Bible, God and this Jesus I had only heard of or known peripherally in my life.

I took notes, writing down everything, the verses and commentary by the minister, trying to soak it all in; but I was plagued by headaches and an ill feeling in general. I requested Tylenol, the only medication allowed to inmates, but it was slow to arrive. I was really suffering physically and emotionally, and I had no idea what was wrong with me. I was clear of drugs and eating better, gaining some weight, but still, something wasn't right.

I muddled through the first six months of my incarceration, attending chapel services, praying and reciting verses, seeking answers and direction for my life. And though I had tried to focus and learn, truly desiring to change, nothing had shaken me and grabbed hold of my soul like the special guests that arrived one Sunday.

Five pretty women (of all ages) were seated on the small stage as I entered to take a seat in a pew near the back, and I looked at them curiously. The minister stood and began speaking:

"Ladies and gentlemen, we have some special guests with us today, five women from the Teen Challenge program (for adults and juveniles as well up to 70 yrs.' old) who are here to share their testimony about how God has changed their lives. Please give them a warm welcome."

This was a new wrinkle. We had not had guest speakers before. I applauded politely, along with the rest of the small crowd, and settled in to listen.

The first speaker stepped confidently to the podium, her eyes sweeping the room and landing on mine briefly. I stared at her raptly as she began.

"Hi, my name is _________, and I am here today to share with you my new hope in Christ, how He has changed my life and rescued me from drugs and the demons of insecurity and self-loathing that were trying to destroy me. I wasn't always who you see on this stage today. Two years ago, I was a drug addict, and crack cocaine was my poison."

That got my attention. I sat up in my seat, listening intently. This woman, well dressed and speaking fluently on stage, looking so healthy and normal, had been a *crack addict*? I had to hear more, and she obliged.

"I came from a broken home. My parents divorced when I was eight years old, and I saw my babysitter or grandparents more than I saw my parents."

She went on to talk about how she was once molested by an uncle, and the impact that event had on her, the downward turn her life took, the first time she used, how quickly she became addicted, and how she became a thief and a liar (a monster)to acquire the drugs she needed.

"And I eventually sold my body for money to buy drugs. Some of you understand what I'm talking about."

Boy, *did* I! I was actually trembling as I listened to her story unfold. The similarities to my own life, in certain aspects, were astounding to me.

"There was nowhere for me to turn," the gal continued. "My mother and father had given up on me after several failed rehab stints. One evening I met Leanne Goff, the Women's Director at Teen Challenge in this area. She's here tonight (Leanne, seated at the end of the row, nods her head and smiles), and she told me about one who loved me, in spite of all I had done, and how I could be clean in body and free in mind. Now, I had gone to church from time to time as a child, before my parents divorced and then with my grandparents. I had *heard* about Jesus - I knew the Christmas and Easter stories - I had *heard* messages from the Bible, but I had never really *listened*. And I remember what Leanne said to me that first night. She said, "If you'll *listen* to me - not *hear* me, okay? - I don't want you to *hear* what I am saying, I want you to *listen* to what

I am saying, what Jesus is saying to you. Listen with your heart and soul, and God will forgive you and save you. 2 Corinthians 5:17 says, *Therefore, if anyone is in Christ, he is a new creation. The old has passed away; behold, the new has come.*

I was feverishly writing that verse down as she recited it - the old passed away? The new has come? What did that mean? I didn't know for sure but it sounded awfully exciting! That I could be "new" after all I had done?

"And the same is true for any of you," the gal said, pointing at her audience. "Would you like to know more?"

I do! I do! I wanted to jump out of my seat and scream. But there were four more speakers to go, and I wanted to hear, no, *listen to,* them all.

The next one had been a stripper, then someone totally normal, at least among the present crowd - she was a housewife and mother who had gotten hooked on painkillers, Oxycodone, and progressed to heroin.

"We are all equal in the eyes of God," she said, "equally sinners and equal to be granted grace. As the Bible says, "For all have sinned and fallen short of the glory of God.""

When they finished, the minister asked any of us that wanted to learn more about the Teen Challenge program to speak with one of the ladies afterward, and as soon as he said, "Amen," I bounced up out my seat and practically ran toward the stage.

CHAPTER 65

I gained an audience with Leanne Goff.

"Hi!" she greeted, smiling sweetly. "And your name is?"

"I'm Shannon!" I blurted. "I want to know more! How do I get to the place where you are? How do I start?" I was so anxious to understand.

"Well, Shannon, the Teen Challenge program is twelve to eighteen months," she informed me, "and it's based on biblical principles. It's not easy; it's much harder than being in here. You have to work and study, but anything worth having is worth working for, right? Listen, the waiting list is long, but here's my card. Pray hard about it! God will make a way for you if it's His will."

She had to get to others, and I stepped aside to allow them their turn.

Back in my cell, I stared at Leanne's card as I sat cross legged on my cot. I was so impressed with her and all the women on that stage. I didn't know how I would get into the program, but I knew I wanted to change, even as I heard the whispering temptation of addiction, that evil voice I wanted to silence forever. At that moment I resolved in my heart to never return to drugs or the dark life I had led.

I fell on my knees, and then put my face to the floor, in an act of utter contrition and humility before God.

"Please forgive me and change me, Oh God!" I wailed, tears pouring from eyes and pooling on the concrete floor of my cell. "Please change me inside, this mess I've made of our huge cell life!" I felt a palpable thirst in my soul for life giving waters, something that would cleanse me and make me feel okay with myself, to know that I'd been forgiven.

When I arose, I collapsed in exhaustion on my bed. I knew, as I lay there breathing hard in that moment, that I was not done with this fight, that the voices which had haunted me over the years would not go quietly into the night. But after meeting and hearing those women on stage today, I now knew it *could* be done, that I *could* overcome, with God's help.

I prayed to Him to show me the way, to lead me and guide me as I fell off to sleep.

CHAPTER 66

For the next two months, I attended chapel every chance I got and bugged the minister about the Teen Challenge program.

"The most important thing you can do, Shannon, is surrender your heart to Christ," he would say. "You know you're most likely facing many years in prison, but you can have Jesus with you every step of the way."

I had told him about my extensive record after the women gave their testimonies that day.

"I know, but I want to get in the program, do the twelve months there," I said earnestly. "I'll do the rest of my time. I'm guilty, so that's how it is, but I want to go through that program."

He put and arm around my shoulder. "I believe you're sincere Shannon. So many in here aren't, but I can feel a humble spirit in you."

I thanked him and went back to my cell to pray before lunch. I got down on my knees, my forehead to the floor, even though it hurt me to do so. I had continued writing requests for Tylenol due to my head and body aches, but as always, the system was notoriously slow, and I just had to live with the pain. I would not stop getting down on my knees and praying to God though, no matter how it hurt, and I found my mindset changing as I prayed. Daily I felt more determined, and a stronger will to resist temptation.

But physically, it seemed I was getting sicker and sicker, as the days went by and my court date came nearer. One night, just a few days before my sentencing, I lay in bed, under a sheet, shivering, my stomach aching and nauseous, alternately sweating and chilling. I felt like I was going to die, and I sung, under my breath, in a shaky, reedy voice the only gospel song I could remember:

What can wash away my sins? Nothing but the blood of Jesus. What can make me whole again? Nothing but the blood of Jesus.

"Oh God," I whispered in prayer, shaking as I clung to the wet sheet, "I'm so sorry for all the wrong things I've done. Please forgive me and help me, you're all I have." I finally fell into a fitful sleep, drifting in and out of consciousness.

I didn't realize it then, but my physical symptoms were manifestations of my soul yearning for God, the casting out of the old, the cleansing of my spirit. Years of desperation, insecurity, loneliness, pain and indifference were being washed away, replaced with the grace of God through Jesus Christ.

I would make it through that touch and go night, struggling within, fighting to live - and when morning came, I would awake a new creation, the old having passed away, because the new had come.

CHAPTER 67

On the day I was to be escorted to the courthouse for sentencing, my court appointed attorney came to my cell for consultation. I had not seen his face one single time over the past nine months. He had no idea what I had been through, had offered me nothing in the way of counsel or hope. My only hope now was in God to move the hearts and minds of men, not this lawyer who would rather be doing something else.

"So, how are we Shannon?" he asked politely.

"I'm fine," I replied, smiling, and he looked at me curiously, wondering, I'm sure, why on earth I would be smiling and calm with fourteen charges facing me.

"Well, that's good," he said, digging some papers out of his briefcase. "Let's talk about how..."

"We don't need to talk about anything."

He raised his eyebrows. "Excuse me?"

"I haven't seen you once since I got here. I know what I've done, I understand the charges against me, and I believe I'll be better off talking for myself than you doing it."

"Shannon, that's not a good idea at all," he responded in a patronizing tone. "Self-representation almost always fails."

"I'll take my chances," I said.

After making that obligatory argument (and not much of one at that; I'm sure he was eager to get to a round of golf), he accepted my proposal and accompanied me to the courthouse to make it official in front of the Honorable Judge Harris.

My step dad, Gordon Howard, made it to my hearing, and he waved and smiled when I entered the courtroom. I returned his salute with a full heart, happy to have a family member in attendance to hear my plea. When my name was called, I stood and faced the judge, along with my soon to be dismissed attorney.

"Mrs. Givazio," the judge began, looking at my rap sheet (a long read), and then over his reading glasses at me.

"Your Honor, may I speak?" I said.

He gave my attorney a quizzical look, then back at me.

"Go ahead."

"I do not wish to be represented by this man. I am waiving my right to an attorney."

"I would strongly advise against that, Mrs. Givazio."

"Thank you, Your Honor. But I would still like to waive my right to an attorney."

Judge Harris looked sharply at my court appointed, and he shrugged, as if to say, "I tried, really I did!"

"Okay. Well then, Counselor, you're dismissed. I'm sure you're broken hearted. Run along."

The charges against me were then read off, eight misdemeanors and six felonies, and when the list was completed, the judge looked at me and sighed.

"How to you plead, Mrs. Givazio?"

"Guilty, Your Honor," I replied, "guilty of it all."

He looked at me with a surprised expression. "You do understand the seriousness of the charges against you?"

"Yes sir," I replied, "and I'm guilty of all of them. But I would like to make a statement before you sentence me please."

"You're certainly entitled to that. Go ahead when you're ready."

I was not a good speaker and I was very nervous at such a major juncture in my life, but I had God and the truth on my side, and that was enough.

"Your Honor, I told you I was guilty of every single charge against me, and it's true. I was addicted to crack cocaine during all of those crimes. I didn't know anything else, didn't care about anything else. Not even two babies I had during those years could take my focus off drugs," I said sincerely, and tears began flowing down my face, but I went on. "Then, about three months ago, I went to chapel and heard these women tell their stories; they had been drug addicts and prostitutes like me! And now they were clean and sober! They told me about a twelve-month program in Teen Challenge, and told me to pray about it, and so I have been, every day and night. It's a long waiting list, but if you will court order me into the program I will get in. I'm asking you to do that please. I just want to go through that program, and you can sentence me to all the years you want to stack on me after that! I'm willing to pay for my crimes, all of them, but please let me go through the program first so I can learn about Jesus and how to live a clean and sober life." My eyes were clouded by tears, so I couldn't see the judge's reaction to my words. "Something radical has happened to me, Your Honor. I'm not the same person I was, and I'm trusting God to help me the rest of the way."

I bowed my head and waited for the judge's ruling, praying he would sentence me first to Teen Challenge.

And then he spoke: "Mrs. Givazio, I've heard a lot of jailhouse religions before, but I believe you are truly sincere. I'm going to release you today, on your own recognizance. Go find a bed with Teen Challenge, and come back to see me in November." He banged the gavel. There were audible gasps in the courtroom at this extraordinary mercy bestowed on me, and I was stunned.

"Thank you, Your Honor!" I cried in amazement. I looked back at my dad and he was coming around to me, his arms out, hugging me.

"Shannon, I can't believe it!" he said in my ear, and nor could I. It was a miracle. The judge had just released me from sentencing on fourteen charges, six of them federal!

"God is great!" I exclaimed, and, looking over my dad's shoulder, I saw the judge nod at me and smile.

CHAPTER 68

I had to be taken back to the correctional center to be processed and released. It would take a couple of hours, and Gordon informed me he had to go to work, so my mother would be coming to pick me up.

After the paperwork, the last thing was handing back over the belongings taken from me upon my arrival there nine months ago: the money, my purse and the clothes I had been wearing before the orange jumpsuit.

I went into the women's restroom to change, and as I pulled on the pants, I remembered something: there was a zipper on the side leg, and hidden in that pocket, if it was still there, was a miniature crack pipe. I unzipped the compartment (unaware I was holding my breath) and there it was. I removed the small pipe, recalling that I had planned to smoke whatever resin was in the bowl when I got bonded out, not realizing then I wouldn't be able to and would spend the next nine months in jail.

The resin was still there, and I knew it would smoke and give me a little high – maybe more than that, I'd been off for so long. I stared at the pipe, the bowl where I used to place the rock, and seriously contemplated it. After all I had been through, the temptation was *still* there - I admit it. I was scared and trembling as the old voice spoke up, trying to tell me it would be okay, *just one, just one more time and that's it, okay?.*

But where I was using drugs, trying to escape my past and those voices, going through it alone, my heavenly Father was now with me. It was His voice I heard then, drowning out all others, and I would listen to Him from that day forward the rest of my life. I was done with drugs; that was what the old me did.

The new me flushed the pipe down the toilet and walked out of jail, free in body and spirit.

CHAPTER 69

As I exited the facility, I saw my mother sitting in her car, waiting for me. When she spotted me approaching, she jumped out, went around to the trunk, opened it and tossed her pocket book inside.

"You think I'm crazy?" she exclaimed. "I'm not going to let you steal my purse and run off!"

I chuckled and shook my head. I didn't blame her in the least for her wariness. She had only known the old me - the lying, thieving drug addict. Only time would inform her of the change Christ had wrought in me.

My mother took me back to her house, and as soon as possible I contacted Teen Challenge, speaking with Shirley Helle, the wife of Teen Challenge Chattanooga Director, Roger Helle. I told her the judge had released me without sentencing, and instructed me to get a bed at Teen Challenge, and then come back in November and see him.

"Shannon, we want you with us, but we have no beds available, and the waiting list is very long," Shirley said.

"But I need to be there!" I exclaimed. "I know God wants me there!"

"Then pray to Him about it," she advised.

And I did, petitioning God morning, noon and night. I studied the Gideon Bible I received in jail daily (a shout out here to Gideon, a wonderful organization that have freely spread the Good News to jails, hotels, hospitals, etc., consistently since 1908!), posing questions to my mother when they came up. She had been a Christian for many years, and was very helpful to me in that time.

My mother took note that I wasn't asking to borrow the car or calling my old party friends. I was content to stay home, out of the way of temptation, and study my Bible, my behavior in stark contrast to that of times past.

"Shannon, you really *have* changed, haven't you?" she said to me one day as I sat on the porch swing. Apparently, she had been watching and listening to me for a bit as I talked to God aloud.

"Yes, I have mom," I replied serenely. "I can't explain it, but it's real in my heart."

She smiled, and it was one of relief as she dared to dream the nightmare of her wayward daughter was finally over.

CHAPTER 70

September 1998:

I spent that typically hot month of August praying to my newfound Savior and blessed hope Jesus for a spot at Teen Challenge. I was not deterred or swayed from my direction, believing with all of my heart that the Lord would respond and help me somehow.

And as August gave way to September, my answer came in the form of a phone call from Leanne Goff.

"Shannon, are you still interested in a bed at Teen Challenge?"

"Yes!" I shrieked.

"Well, we have a bed available. How soon can you come?"

"Today, *now*, if you'll take me!" I cried, thankfulness flooding my soul.

"Well absolutely! I love your enthusiasm Shannon! We'll see you soon."

We rang off and I jumped up and down, laughing and crying, hollering, "Thank you Jesus!" at the top of my lungs. I was so overwhelmed with joy that God had answered my prayer, and I knew from that day forward I could depend on Him and trust Him, that He would *never* let me down. He was the one I had been searching for all of my life - the void in my soul, the cup that would quench my thirst, the bread that would fill my hunger. No drug, no man, no person could do that for me, and I was sure then that I would *never* leave Him!

"Shannon, what's this all about?" my mother asked, coming from the other room.

"They have a bed for me!" I exclaimed, tears pouring down my face. "God made a way!"

She hugged me tightly, crying along with me, and later helped me pack to begin the next chapter in my life, my journey through the Teen Challenge program.

CHAPTER 71

Before I arrived at Teen Challenge, I had imagined the instructors and teachers there to be solemn and strict in disposition, maybe dressed in habits like Nuns.

That presumption was proved wrong from the moment I met Soraya Rivas at the entrance way. She was a very pretty, dark haired Columbian woman, around my age at the time I guessed (thirtyish), and she spoke in such a calm voice, with a most captivating smile.

"Welcome to Teen Challenge, Shannon," she greeted, "please follow me."

In a small, nondescript room, Soraya began my orientation, explaining the rules in her tranquil voice.

"No loud stuff here, you understand," she said. "We conduct ourselves properly, in an orderly fashion based on biblical principles. We don't talk about or glamorize our past lives. That life is over and gone. If you have an open heart, God will change you here."

My heart couldn't be more open, and I sat in amazement listening to Soraya. She was at peace with herself, serene yet confident, and so graceful in manner and speech. I wanted to be *just* like her.

"Everyone is assigned a counselor," she continued.

"Who's mine?"

"Me," she replied.

I was thrilled! My instant role model would be my counselor, my teacher!

"Anytime you need to talk, Shannon, feel free to knock on my door. I am here for you, okay?"

"Yes! Thank you!"

After signing papers, I was taken to the room where I would be spending at least the next eight months. I met my roommates: Mag, a sixty-year-old black woman whose poison, like me, had been crack cocaine, and Kris, a heroin addict. Kris had been in the program for nine months, and she was now in the reentry phase where she could look for a job, get her own room in the Teen Challenge facility - when she could afford it - and other privileges.

After I got settled in, we sat on our beds - sucking on Dum-Dum lollipops - while my two new friends explained the program.

"So, this ain't no walk in the park honey," Mag said. "First four months, you gonna wish you were back in the poke." Kris chuckled at that, probably remembering her pass through that phase. "Yeah, you're going to study, do chores, study, do chores, take exams, and study...you get the picture," Kris said, waving a hand in the air. She was a skinny thing with chopped off hair, sort of nervous acting, eyes darting about the room when she talked.

"Then you go into training, where I'm at, four to eight months," Mag said. "Lots of classes on relationships, etiquette, stuff like that. You can earn privileges in this phase."

"What's that mean?" I asked.

"Well, like you can get two cups of coffee in the morning instead of just one," Mag said. "But you gotta earn it!"

"That's right," Kris agreed, nodding. "And never more than two cups of coffee per day! Got to keep the mood-altering substances to a minimum!"

We all shared a laugh before Kris continued.

"Then at nine months, if you phase up and pass all your tests, you get to look for a job and rent your own room here, like me."

"How's that going?" I asked.

"She ain't tryin'!" Mag said, winking at me. "She don't wanna leave Mamma Mag!"

"You know it!" Kris replied, putting an arm around Mag's shoulder and hugging her cheek to cheek.

I would get to know them both so much better before they left the program, as we shared our struggles, hopes and dreams. Kris would be first to graduate, and on the day she left, when she hugged my neck, I saw a haunted look in her eyes, that fear of being on her own, away from the program.

"I love you girl!" I whispered in her ear as I hugged her tight. "Trust God and stay clean, you hear? He's the only one that can help you through!"

"I got this!" she replied.

But she didn't. A year later, Kris would die from a drug overdose, another heartbreaking case of an addict going clean then going back...

...and then going away forever.

CHAPTER 72

I assimilated into the Teen Challenge program day by day, learning at every step how to conduct myself. Although initially challenging, I found the results within myself so rewarding that the difficulties seemed nothing in comparison.

One memorable teachable moment occurred early in the first phase (0-4 months). There were various chores assigned each week, and I was put on the cooking schedule, along with several other girls. My job was to cut carrots for the evening meal, and as I busily performed my duty, in an efficient manner (or so I thought), I was approached by Sandra, our class instructor.

"Shannon, you want me to show you a different way to do that?"

Now, I had experienced the grace of God, salvation of my soul through Jesus Christ, make no mistake. I had kicked drugs out of my life and turned over a new leaf; but I was a work in progress, like every new Christian, and as long as we are on this earth we have to deal with our defensive, selfish natures.

"I *know how* to cut carrots!" I responded in a smart aleck tone, rolling my eyes. I continued working, and I heard her whisper gently in my ear:

"Can I talk to you in the other room for a moment?"

Oops! Once in the room, she took a chair and offered me a seat, and I sat across from her. I was in trouble, and now would come the appropriate sentence, something like a week confined to my room, or lashings, I had no idea.

"Shannon, we don't talk to each other like that around here," she said with a smile. "I was just offering my help, and you bit my head off. We don't do that, do you understand?"

She *was* rebuking me, but in a loving and kind way. I had never experienced that, and it blew my mind. I did not feel the need to defend myself; rather, I got it, it was my mouth to blame, I just needed to control my tongue.

"Yes mam," I replied sincerely.

"Think *before* you speak," Sandra advised, and then stood, and I followed suit. "You're going to do just fine here Shannon."

"Thank you so much! Now, will you show me how to cut carrots?"

The relationship class, one of many in the program, taught the difference between acquaintances, casual and close friends, and that close friends should be nurtured and strengthened.

There was a right and wrong way to do everything, and I learned the differences in my time there. Each facet of life was addressed, from social skills to the professional, as well as positive personal habits.

Soraya Rivas and Sandra were two extremely inspirational role models to me throughout the program. I admired and wanted to emulate them, to speak as they did and have the same loving, kind hearts. I could not imagine two better examples of a Christ-like spirit, and I am forever grateful to them for helping guide me through, and prepare me for life beyond, the program.

In November, I went back to court and reported to Judge Harris, as I had been ordered.

"Well, Shannon, I see you found a bed at Teen Challenge."

"Yes, I have, Your Honor!"

"And you are applying yourself, I take it?"

"Oh yes sir!" I exclaimed. "I love it there! I've learned so much already!"

He looked at me over his reading glasses and smiled. "Very well. I hereby order you to complete the Teen Challenge program, Shannon. All charges against you in my court will be dropped, contingent on your completing the program, of course."

"Oh, I will, Your Honor!"

"I've no doubt about it," he replied.

"Thank you, thank you!"

CHAPTER 73

"Soraya, I have a question," I asked my counselor one evening as I neared the end of my first four months in the program.

I had been clean and sober for thirteen months, and I was certain as I could be that I would never return to my former life. With that thought, I had been wondering how I could get out of my marriage to Jimmy. I was a totally different person now, and I could see no way forward for us.

"Go ahead Shannon," she replied.

"Well, I really trust you Soraya, and I want to tell you about my marriage and my husband." I went on to fill her in on my mistreatment at his hands, the physical and verbal abuse I endured for so long.

"But the Bible says you can't get a divorce, right?" I concluded. "So, I'm stuck."

"No, that's not true at all, Shannon," Soraya said. "We believe God doesn't recognize marriage between couples not blessed by Him. If He had no part in it, and from what you're telling me He was nowhere near it, then you need to get a divorce and get it right!"

"Really?" I couldn't believe what I was hearing. "But you'll have to hire your own divorce lawyer when you can, we can't do that for you."

"I understand!" I replied. "Thank you for making that clear to me!" I hugged her neck and she embraced me in return.

"You're making good progress here Shannon. I am so proud of you! Keep up the good work!"

Hearing her say that made me feel so good, and I strove harder every day to grow in spirit and in truth.

CHAPTER 74

Just before I completed the first phase of the program, I was informed I was eligible to participate in a mission trip to San Luis Potosi, Mexico, early in the second phase.

I had to raise my own money for the trip. No asking family members for funds, but I could hit up friends and acquaintances. Also, by that point some other girls and I were going around to churches, giving our testimonies. The first time I told my story, it wasn't lost on me that I had reached a place I had dreamed of that day in jail when I was so moved by those wonderful women giving their declarations of faith.

During those services, church members would be handed envelopes with our names inscribed on the front, and whoever touched their heart the most would receive that person's donation. I was fortunate enough to be gifted some, and along with donations from some of my mother's clients (I called her and told her about my exciting trip and she went right to work raising money for me...thanks Mom!), I had enough for a ticket.

I had to take a Spanish language class before we went, and I became fairly fluent in a few phrases. While there, we visited hospitals, jails and neighborhoods, proclaiming as best we could the saving grace of God. It was eye opening to witness the squalid living conditions endured by most - dirt floors, children in their bare feet with no shoes to wear. I would hold their hands and pray with them, and many came to Christ during our visit.

I went on a second trip to New Orleans during Mardi Gras, and *that* was different. I had been taught by Teen Challenge that *anywhere my feet took me I was representing the Kingdom of God* and to always be vigilant concerning my actions and words. That doctrine was put to the test in the Big Easy, as party goers spit in my face and were rude in general to me and my male partner (all of the girls were paired with a male for safety). We soldiered on, however, and persevered through adversity, continuing to present our beliefs and the opportunity to anyone who wanted to join us and accept Christ.

Overall, it wasn't as successful as San Luis Potosi, but we did hand out some tracts and plant some seeds. While there, we were coordinated by the Urban Missions of New Orleans, and the director dutifully pitched the school to us. I was very interested in it, and was something I really wanted to do after I graduated, but the tuition for the two-year school was seven thousand dollars.

At that time, it was just a dream.

CHAPTER 75

During the training phase (4-8 months) there were many classes, and I soaked in everything I could. There were etiquette classes - where I learned how to set a table and how to eat at that set table - classes on stewardship, where I learned how to divide and section money, a certain percentage for savings, for groceries, etc. In general, techniques and knowledge for every possible occasion in one's life. But most importantly, we were taught that God hears us when we talk to Him, that He was interested in our lives and wanted to be involved in it every second of every day.

Soraya, my counselor, was always ready to talk or help me in whatever way she could.

"Shannon," she told me one day, "I know someday you'll want to be the wife of a good, Christian man. You'll get clear of your current situation, and when you are, God will lead you to the one. If I were you, I would make a list of the qualities I'm looking for in a man, and pray to God concerning him, that He would bless and keep him for you."

So, I made the list, and throughout my stay in Teen Challenge, I prayed over it daily:

"God, I know my future husband, the one meant for me, is in the world today. Please protect him and bless him, and meet every need he has until you bring us together."

Although I didn't know how it would all go down, I had faith it would come to be, and I looked forward to meeting him.

There was a special trip planned for the staff and students that year to the Brownsville revival in Pensacola, Florida. The revival had begun in 1995, when evangelist Steve Hill took the pulpit on Father's Day, asking at the end of the otherwise normal service if anyone in the audience desired, "a fresh touch from God?" That question sparked many to come forward that day, and people continued to flock to that church in the subsequent years. The day I was there, I heard Steve and his wife Jeri preach, and it was an eye opening, incredible experience. I bought their CD's, filled with sermons and helpful instruction, and listened to them every chance I got while at Teen Challenge and beyond. Their messages had a tremendous impact on my Christian life, and helped shape me into the person I am today.

I had changed so much from the person I was when I entered the Teen Challenge program five months earlier that my mother was shocked when she came to visit me. Gone was the girl I had been, the bad attitude, and even my speech had changed.

"Amazing," she remarked after we spent some time together. "This program is *really* something. Can you come back here if you relapse again?"

I chuckled at that. I'd failed and disappointed her so many times before, she couldn't grasp the idea I would never return to the old Shannon I was.

"I don't plan on relapsing Mom," I said evenly, smiling. "I don't need drugs anymore. I have God, and that's enough."

She looked into my eyes, and must have seen something she believed in because she squeezed my neck hard in the next instant.

"Oh, Shannon, I've prayed for this for so many years!"

"Thank you, Mom," I said sincerely.

Gordon had come with her, my wonderful step father who was a father to me in all respects. I remembered how he had went out of his way to hunt me down, when I was working the streets in Chattanooga, so out of his element, a good man from a small town - but he bravely drove those mean streets, among the drug dealers, prostitutes and gangs, looking for me, just to talk or take me somewhere to eat.

I hugged him tightly.

"I love you, Dad," I said, a tear rolling down my cheek, and when we pulled apart, I saw a tear on his cheek too.

"I love you too, Shannon. I've always believed you would come around."

Visiting time came to an end, and I went back to my life in the program. For the next three months, I continued growing and learning under the tutelage of Soraya Rivas and Instructor Sandra, as well as her helpful and precious husband Quinby, until the day came, at eight months, when I was to begin my reentry into society.

Now I would go out looking for a job and head back into the real world.

With God as my helper, I was ready.

CHAPTER 76

I had completed eight months in the Teen Challenge program, and the effect on my life, spiritually, mentally and physically was readily apparent. And even though I had put on some weight and my skin and eyes had cleared up, I still felt, when I began working, someone may recognize me in public, so I cut my hair short (shoulder length - it had been three quarters down my back),and forewent make-up.

There were some ground rules that were gone over with me before I went on my hunt: I had to bring back proof each day, in the form of a letter signed by the prospective employer, that I had actually applied for a job, and should I attain employment, I had to keep receipts for everything I purchased (lunch, drinks etc.).

The accountability, in expenditures and studies as I assimilated back into society, were designed to keep me grounded and tethered even as I enjoyed increased freedoms and responsibility. It is a gradual process and extremely successful as Teen Challenge boasts an 87% success rate among graduates, one of the highest in the world.

If you are reading this book and need proven, effective help overcoming your addictions, I encourage you to find a Teen Challenge facility and enter the program. If you go into Teen Challenge with an open heart and mind, you'll have the best chance, in my opinion, to finally be free of the substances that are destroying you and your relationships. It worked for me.

A local grocery store was the first stop on my job search (I had experience in that field), and I was nervous as I entered. I had been out of society for so long, but I squared my shoulders as best I could and approached a man wearing a shirt and tie. He looked like he was in charge.

"Can I help you?" he asked as he counted the number of registers open, stabbing a finger in the air.

"Yes, I'm looking for a job."

When he turned his attention to me, I recognized him as a guy I had attended high school with.

"Chris?"

"Yes, that's me," he said, and then recognition dawned on his face. "We went to school together, right?"

"That's right! I'm Shannon Gi...well, would have been Parker back then."

"I remember you. So, you're looking for a job?"

"Yes. Just wondered if you had anything."

"Hey, I'm always looking for good help!" he said. "Come on back and let's get you an application." He led me to his office and placed the form on a clipboard, handing it, and a pen, to me. "Take your time, Shannon. Leave it there on my desk and I'll get in touch with you, okay?"

"Okay. Thanks!"

Chris and I had been just passing acquaintances in school, but the familiarity, given my jitters, was still nice.

When I got to the question on the application about felonies and arrests, I wrote: *I need to talk to you about this.*

On the way out, I remembered the "proof" letter I needed him to sign.

"What's this about?" he asked when I presented the form to him.

"I'm in a program, and I have to prove I'm looking for a job," I said. It was going to come out some time. He raised his eyebrows. "I hope you'll give me a chance, Chris. I'm a changed person and I need this."

"Okay Shannon," he said smiling and signing the form. "I'll be in touch."

I walked out of the store and paused in the parking lot, looking up at the gray sky and taking a deep breath of the chilly, February air. It was God's guidance that Chris, a man I knew from my past, was the manager at the first place I put in. I believed it, because I believed God had a hand in my life, in every step along the way.

CHAPTER 77

The very next morning, Chris called me back in for an interview.

"So, you wanted to talk about this?" he said, as we were seated in his office.

"Yes, thanks for giving me the opportunity," I said. I went on to tell him everything - my drug addiction, arrests and my salvation and success with Teen Challenge. "I don't miss my old life at all. I am looking forward to the rest of my life as a clean and sober Christian."

He was staring at me, a look of wonder in his eyes, and after an extended pause he cleared his throat and stood, smiling broadly.

"When can you start Shannon?"

"Now!" I replied, clapping my hands together in joy and saying a thank you prayer to Jesus in my heart.

"Well, let's get you going then!"

After orientation, I spent my first day in training to be a cashier. I was excited about the opportunity, not only to make a living but also to interact with people and find subtle ways to talk to them about Christ. Teen Challenge asks that all those going through reentry into society attempt to broach the subject of Jesus and the Christian life to at least three people per day, in a restrained, respectful manner.

After I started, I made an effort to smile and be friendly to everyone, and I always said, "God bless you," when they left my line, or "God loves you," depending on the person or the circumstances. Often, these phrases would lead to conversations with fellow Christians and would create opportunities to talk to those who had not experienced the Christian life.

There were so many wonderful people that came through my line, and I tried to have a positive impact on their short time with me, by smiling and offering words of encouragement and simply engaging and taking an interest in their lives. I had opportunities to talk about the Teen Challenge program, often to grandmothers or mothers whose children were hooked on drugs and had failed rehab many times, and I hope any of those I spoke to found the help they needed.

I was especially thrilled to meet couples that came through the line with small children. I was, of course, remembering my children, Tiffany and Allison, and vicariously interacting with them in others.

I had not been long on the job when I noticed an older black man who came in at the same time every day. He would buy only a Wall Street Journal, and paid for his paper with a scowl, never speaking a word to anyone. My fellow employees told me he had a reputation as a mean old man, and had been coming into the store for his morning paper since its opening. He had no set line he went through, but when he chose mine, I saw it as a challenge to try and get a rise out of him.

"Good morning!" I would greet him with a wide smile. "How are you today sir?" The first couple of times, my exuberant greeting elicited zero responses, but one morning, he actually *grunted*. Not a *word*, mind you, but a sound nonetheless! I was making progress!

"You must be the kind of man who likes an ordered life!" I said to him another morning, just throwing things against the wall, seeing if anything would stick.

"My name is Glover," he said, and I froze as I was ringing him up. What? Did the notoriously grumpy, mean man just speak to me?

"What did you say?" I had been so shocked to hear actual words issuing forth from his lips I missed what he said.

"Glover," he repeated. "If you insist on addressing me every morning, use my name please."

"Absolutely, Mr. Glover!" I exclaimed. "See you tomorrow morning then!"

He nodded, and, tucking his paper under his arm, he looked at me and...smiled, a small one, but it was definitely a *smile*.

As he went out the door, my own smile almost broke my face.

CHAPTER 78

There was a second mission trip to San Luis Potosi planned at the midway point of my reentry phase, so I busied myself raising funds again. There were the church visits and donations, plus I was making money now and saving a lot of it. A drug free life, better in *every* respect, is also much less expensive!

I was so enjoying my job at the grocery store. I wanted people to see the light of love in my eyes, and hear it in my voice and words. Many of them sought my line when it was time to check out, including Mr. Glover, who, as it turned out, had a nice guy living inside of him.

"How are you doing today, Mr. Glover?" I beamed, and he returned it with his now customary grin.

"Fine Shannon, how are you?"

"I'm blessed!" I replied.

"I hear you."

He gave me the money for the paper and I rang it up.

"Mr. Glover, if you're a Christian, I hope you'll pray for me."

"Well, I am and I will," he responded, an actual look of concern in his eyes. "Everything okay?"

"Oh yes! I'm just going on another mission trip to Mexico soon, and I need to raise a little more money for it. The last time we were able to win a lot of souls for Christ there. It was great!"

"Sounds like a good thing," he said. "Have a good day, Shannon!"

"You too, Mr. Glover! God Bless you!"

The next day Mr. Glover came through my line as usual, but this time he slid an envelope into my hand.

"For your mission trip, Shannon," he said.

I opened the envelope and counted out five one hundred-dollar bills.

"Oh Mr. Glover!" I cried, running around my register and embracing him, hugging his neck tightly. "God bless you! Thank you!"

He chuckled and awkwardly returned my gesture. "You're welcome, hon. Hope that helps."

I now had my own room at Teen Challenge, and later that evening, after my prayers, I reflected on where I was in the program, as well as my spiritual and personal life. I had longed to be like Soraya Rivas and Sandra - kind, peaceful women who exuded the spirit of Christ every moment of their lives. I felt I was finally becoming like them, as indicated by the customers who now sought me out - our warm and genuine interactions - and it was a truly beautiful thing.

The drug addicted prostitute was long gone, replaced by a new creature in Christ, and I knew none of the people I met in the grocery store would ever imagine in their wildest dreams what I had been.

Such is the life changing power of a relationship with Jesus Christ, and I was never going to look back again.

CHAPTER 79

There were so many marvelous people I encountered working as a cashier at the grocery store, none more so than Mike, who came through my line one day not long before my trip to Mexico.

He was a charismatic man, with the kind of face and smile that made one feel immediately at ease. His voice was rich and resonate, a feature that served him well in his capacity as a stock broker.

"Well how are you today..." a pause as he bent forward and read my name tag, "Shannon!"

"I'm blessed, how are you sir?" I responded, pleasantly surprised by his personality.

"The same! I'm Mike."

"So good to meet you!"

"Where are you from?" he asked.

"A small town not far from here. Right now I live in a room at Teen Challenge. Have you ever heard of it?"

"Teen Challenge? Why yes, I've supported them for years! It's a great organization!"

"Yes it is!" I agreed. "So what do you do Mike?"

"I'm a stock broker," he replied, "do a little trading here and there."

"If you've supported Teen Challenge, I'd assume you're a Christian?"

"You'd be right!" he affirmed.

"Well, I hope you'll pray for me then. I'm going on a second mission trip to Mexico next week!"

"That's great! I'll certainly do that. It was good to meet you Shannon!"

"You too Mike! God Bless you!"

My boss was accommodating, allowing me time off for the mission trip, and two days before our group left Chattanooga for Mexico, Leanne Goff informed me that Mike had mailed a two-hundred-dollar check to Teen Challenge Chattanooga, and on the memo line had written, *For: Shannon's trip*.

God was guiding me, placing precious, invaluable people in my life to help me along the way, and I am forever grateful to those who heard God's call...and listened.

CHAPTER 80

I had planned to join Urban Missions in New Orleans after Teen Challenge, but the tuition of seven thousand dollars was steep for the two-year school, at least for a cashier. It would take me awhile to save up that much, but I was okay to continue working at the grocery store until I had it.

Both of my new friends had visited the Teen Challenge facilities and had been impressed with the staff and curriculum, especially the success rate of students graduating the program.

I discussed my life and future with the two gentlemen when they came through my line, and both knew of my desire to attend Urban Missions.

"How much is the tuition?" Mike asked me.

"Seven thousand," I replied.

"Got any saved up?"

"Yes, but it will take a while to get the rest. I'm okay though, really. I'm fine here until I get it."

"I know I'd miss you!" he said, and I smiled.

"Thank you, Mike. Same here."

Mr. Glover, for his part, would come through my line and periodically give me fifty or hundred-dollar bills for my move.

"The Crescent City is an expensive place to live," he told me. "I know." I didn't ask him how he knew, just took his word for it.

"Thank you so much for your help, Mr. Glover," I said. "You have been such a blessing to me!"

"And you have to me, Shannon," he replied, smiling.

A week later, Leanne Goff called me into her office, and I took a seat.

"Shannon, what on earth are you doing?" she asked with a concerned look on her face.

I looked at her, perplexed. "What do you mean, Leanne?"

And then she laughed. "I'm just pulling your leg! I called you in here to show you this." She spun a check around on the desk so I could read it:

Teen Challenge...amount $7000...for Shannon's Urban Mission tuition... Michael __________ .

I couldn't believe what I was seeing.

He gave me the *whole* thing," I choked out.

"Yes, dear," Leanne said. "God is working miracles in your life."

But the biggest, most exciting miracle was yet to come.

CHAPTER 81

November 1999:

The holiday season was in full force.

The weeks leading up to Thanksgiving and Christmas are extremely busy times in a grocery store, and though it was exhausting I loved my job, seeing my regulars and meeting new people.

I had graduated from Teen Challenge in September, and I was now two and a half months from the next chapter in my life, the Urban Missions School in New Orleans. Where it would have been another two years or not at all, I was now full steam ahead to start the winter semester due to Mike's incredible gift.

It was a late Friday morning when Gloria, the lady who had handled the adoption of Allison for Bethany Christian Services, came through my line.

I reached across the counter and hugged her neck. "Gloria!" I exclaimed, "oh my goodness!"

"My, my how good you look Shannon!" she said. "It's amazing!"

"I'm in Teen Challenge and I gave my heart to Christ almost two years ago!" I blurted. "I'm drug free!"

"I know," she replied, and I looked at her quizzically. "Shannon, I saw you in here a couple of weeks ago and recognized you. I mean, you look so much different...and better! But I knew it was you. Anyway, I called some people and they told me about your Teen Challenge experience."

"Wow," was all I could manage at that moment. I suddenly realized standing before me was the woman who I had given up my second child to, who had taken her from my arms and out of my life. I didn't blame her at all, but it briefly brought back those voices of condemnation and feelings of guilt. I felt the wind go out of my sails and a storm brewing in my soul. I said an internal prayer for strength, closing my eyes, and then Gloria touched my forearm lightly. I opened my misty eyes and put on a brave smile.

"Do you get a lunch break Shannon? I'd like to visit with you, talk to you."

"Yes, in thirty minutes."

"Do you like the Chinese place next door?"

"Yes, that's fine," I said still trying to emotionally shore myself up.

"I'll see you in thirty minutes then!" Gloria said.

I wasn't sure I could stomach taking lunch with the woman that was involved in that traumatic event in my life. The very sight of her brought back the pitiful person I had been, the regret. No doubt Allison was better off where she was, but oh how I wished I could have been clean and sober during that pregnancy, as I was now! I had put all of that behind me, and now here was a flesh and blood memory associated with the worst day of my life, wanting to talk, and about *what* exactly?

I didn't see the point, but I would go and hear what she had to say until I couldn't take it anymore. I would run out if it got too hard.

So help me I would.

CHAPTER 82

When I entered the restaurant, I saw Gloria had already gotten a table and was waving me over.

I sat and folded my hands in front of me, and she got right to the point.

"Shannon, the couple who adopted your child lives on Lookout Mountain. The mother has come through your line."

"What?" I responded, my mind spinning and my eyes widening, "All...Allison's mother? Her...her adoptive parents?"

"Yes," Gloria confirmed. The mother knew who you were, and she was so impressed with how dramatically you've changed."

She leaned forward and looked into my trembling eyes.

"Shannon, they want to offer you the chance to be a part of your child's life."

"Excuse me a moment," I somehow managed to say as I rose on unsteady legs and staggered toward the women's restroom, through the door and into a stall. I closed the door and collapsed to my knees, tears pouring down my face.

"Oh God thank you, thank you, thank you!" I wailed, my soul crying out, my heart overwhelmed with joy and thanksgiving for the miracle He was bringing about in my life. "My precious Jesus, my Savior thank you from the bottom of my heart!"

I stayed there a full five minutes, weeping in the throes of the grace of God before I hauled myself up.

When I returned to the table, somewhat composed, Gloria looked at my wet, red eyes with concern.

"Are you okay?" she asked.

"Am I okay? I'm going to get to see my baby! I am so grateful to God!"

"I know you are, dear," she replied. "A little bit about them; the father is a doctor, in his forties, and the mother is a stay at home mom with six other children. She's on the board at Bethany Christian Services. They fell in love with Allison and wanted to adopt her as soon as they learned of her availability. They understood there was a chance she may have problems due to your drug use during the pregnancy, but it turns out she is just fine!"

"Praise God!" I exclaimed.

"Indeed! So the parents want to meet with you, Shannon. Isn't that the most amazing thing?"

"It's amazing *grace*," I said sincerely.

We parted ways, with Gloria informing me she would be in touch on a meeting place and time.

I went back to work walking on a cloud and smiling from ear to ear.

CHAPTER 83

A week later, Gloria picked me up for our meeting with the parents, sans Allison, at Bethany Christian Services to discuss the arrangements.

"Shannon!" my daughter's beautiful adoptive mother greeted me as we entered the meeting room, rising and holding out a dozen red roses. "Roses, for the birth mother of our precious Allison."

I took the roses, tears forming in my eyes.

"And a cross necklace, to celebrate your new life."

She clasped the chain around my neck as a tear rolled down my cheek.

"Thank you," I said softly, barely able to speak.

The smiling father approached and addressed me. "Hello Shannon. Good to meet you."

"Thank you," I repeated, all I could think to say, but I really was.

"Well, let's all have a seat," Gloria suggested, and we did, Gloria and I on one side, facing my daughter's adoptive parents.

"Shannon," the mother began, "I just want to say how remarkable your turn around has been. From where you were, it's absolutely amazing!"

"Thank you." I was beginning to sound like a broken record, I know, but I didn't want to say or do anything to hurt my chances. They had the power entirely (someone always does, right?), so I was tiptoeing through the tulips.

"We didn't know if you even wanted to meet your baby, but after seeing how you turned out, your beautiful spirit, we wanted to give you the opportunity."

"I do! I do!" I exclaimed, finally able to summon a different response.

"Wonderful!" she said. "I've brought along some pictures of Allison, if you'd like to see them."

"Yes, I would *love* to see them!"

I was presented photos of Allison from infancy to her current age of twenty months, in a variety of poses and situations. She looked so cute and healthy and I couldn't stop crying as I looked at them, at the time I had missed out on in my daughter's life. I was comforted that she had such wonderful parents and opportunities before her, but in every picture of my daughter and her adoptive mother, I naturally felt the pain of my absence and replacement.

They went over the rules of my visits and phone calls, and we set a date for my first meeting with Allison in two weeks, after Thanksgiving.

We hugged and parted ways, and, needless to say, I was filled with anticipation for the day I would see my little girl.

CHAPTER 84

It was a park where we met, on a gray, cool day in early December. Gloria once again escorted me, and when I stepped out of the car, I saw the doctor, his wife, and my daughter wearing a gorgeous red dress.

She was adorable, and I approached with apprehension, my hands clasped in front of me (trying to control them, as I instinctively wanted to run and sweep her up in my arms).

The mother turned her toward me, pointed and said:

 This is Shannon, and guess what? You used to be in her belly!"

"In hur beweee?" the cutest little thing in the world repeated.

"Yes! So Shannon is our special friend!"

I simply could not believe the selflessness and kindness of the mother to introduce me that way.

"Thank you so much," I whispered, all I could manage.

Tears stung my eyes, and I felt my heart in my throat in the next moment as my daughter came to me, placing her little hand in mine and leading me to the swing sets. The mother nodded her approval, and once there, I lifted her into the seat and gently pushed her, as Gloria, the doctor and his wife stood back, watching and smiling.

It was like a dream as I swung her, looking at her perfect hair, her perfect face; and if it was a dream, I didn't ever want to wake up. But it was real, and a testament to the miraculous work God can do in your life, if you trust and give it all to Him.

When it was time to part, I did with a heavy heart, hugging and telling Allison (her name always to me) I loved her and that she would be seeing more of me.

CHAPTER 85

January 2000:

The Y2K bug that was supposed to cripple the world at the beginning of the new millennium never materialized, but those kinds of things are not the concern of recovering addicts in the Teen Challenge program.

Things like making it day to day are, and I regularly encountered addicts in jails where I gave my testimony, in the same place I was not so long ago, wondering how they were ever going to make it without drugs. Although I had graduated in September of the previous year, I still helped out at Teen Challenge, volunteering my time as much as possible. I was, and am still, so thankful to that organization for all they did for me.

After the reunion with Allison, I put off going to Urban Missions for the winter semester, preferring to spend whatever spare time I had visiting with and getting to know my daughter.

One Sunday, after speaking at a church, I sat beside this friendly lady, and we struck up a conversation. Her name was Ally, and I told her about my daughter, who had the same name. "I was so impressed with your story Shannon," she said. "God has really worked miracles in your life."

"Thank you," I responded. "What do you do, may I ask?"

"I'm an attorney."

Before we parted that day she expressed an interest in getting together for lunch, and we exchanged numbers.

Ally and I became fast friends. She would pick me up at work and take me out to lunch, and on the weekends we would go shopping, all the while getting to know each other better.

The thought of my ill-fated, disastrous marriage to Jimmy Givazio, and how to get out of it, was something that had been on my mind since I became a Christian. One day, during lunch with my new best friend, I mentioned it.

"Do you, by any chance, do divorces?" I asked. I knew from our conversations she was a real estate attorney.

"Yes, I can. Why do you ask?"

"Well, I'm married, Ally," I informed her, and she didn't blink.

"Go ahead."

I went on to explain the circumstances under which Jimmy and I were married, and all of the details (as we girls are want to do).

"And I've changed everything about my life except being married to him!" I finished. "I'm sure he doesn't want to be married to me anymore either."

"Where is he?" she asked.

"In prison."

"No problem. Let's get to work on it," she said, slapping the table lightly.

"How much is it going to cost me?"

"Pro bono honey," she replied. "Let's get you free and clear of that monster."

She got all the paperwork together and mailed it off, and in less than two weeks it came back signed by Jimmy Givazio.

"You'll be divorced and living the single life in six weeks," Ally informed me.

"That's it?"

"Yep."

I squealed with delight and hugged her fiercely. "I can't believe it! Thank you, thank you from the bottom of my heart!"

I truly believe God places people in your life to carry out His will, and Ally was the latest in a long line of people who had helped me along the way since I trusted Christ.

CHAPTER 86

With my divorce out of the way, I turned my attention to the outstanding warrants facing me in Tampa and Atlanta. I had to get those cleared up, and I approached Ally for advice.

"You'll want to get a Shepherd's Guide for those areas," she said.

"What's that?"

"It's a directory with phone numbers of Christian businesses in those places. You'll find a Christian attorney that may take on your case."

I sent off for and received a copy, and Ally helped me secure representation in both cities. Soraya Rivas and Leanne Goff made the trips with me and spoke as character witnesses on my behalf.

All the charges were dropped, and I am eternally grateful to the Christian attorneys who represented me, to Ally for guiding me, and Leanne Goff and Soraya Rivas for taking the time out of their lives to declare for me in court.

How precious it is to know God's grace and to have friends of the faith helping you through life.

CHAPTER 87

My dad, Gordon Howard, began his battle with cancer about the same time I entered the Teen Challenge program. He had not been a religious man up to that point in his life, but when he saw and heard the astounding things taking place in my life early on (the day the judge released me from those felonies and misdemeanors to pursue Teen Challenge, for instance), it began steering his thoughts toward God. When he got sick, he reached out to Christ, accepting Him, and to me, asking that I get my prayer warriors to petition for him.

"I see all the things God has done for you, Shannon. It's been amazing, and I'm so proud of you. It made a believer out of me. And no matter what happens, I'm in God's hands now."

"I'll pray for you, Dad, and get everyone I know to do the same."

"Thanks for that. I love you girl."

But Gordon Howard, that great dad to me and wonderful husband to my mother, went home to be with the Lord on June 7th, 2000.

A few weeks after the funeral, my mother showed up at my studio apartment (I had moved out of my room at Teen Challenge after graduation) driving a Camry.

"It's yours," she told me, after she led me outside. "Gordon left it to you in his will. It's totally paid for and has insurance coverage for a year."

I broke down and cried on the spot, hugging my mother, and she joined in too, an emotional release we both needed. I had not had my own car in a while, and it would bring greater independence.

I was ready.

CHAPTER 88

After my trip to New Orleans early in the program, I had dreamed of attending the Urban Missions School. It would be a different place, a marked change from my past or current life, and that was a large part, if not all, of the attraction. But it was a dream born at a time when I wasn't far removed from my life as an addict, a time when anywhere but where I was sounded good. After Allison came into my life, and the passing of my step father, my enthusiasm for the school began to ebb.

The seven-thousand-dollar tuition had been paid, however, compliments of my friend Mike, and I felt compelled to enroll for the fall semester.

I worked out my notice at the grocery store, said my good-byes to Chris, the store manager, my customers and to all the staff at Teen Challenge, tearful occasions one and all, and I took off driving south.

I lasted two days.

I went to the office of U.M. and explained the situation.

"I don't belong here," I said. "I've made a mistake." I was anxious and felt so out of place.

"Are you using again?" she asked me.

"No, no, this just isn't right for me. It's not God's plan for me, it was *my* plan, I chose this, so it's *wrong*."

"Are you sure about this, Shannon?"

"I couldn't be more sure. And please send Mike's money back to him."

"We will do that," she assured, and as quickly as I could I packed my bags and headed back to Tennessee.

CHAPTER 89

When I got back to Tennessee, I was able to reacquire my studio apartment (they hadn't had time to list it) and my old job.

"That was fast!" Chris exclaimed. "I had a feeling you weren't happy about it, Shannon."

"You were right!"

"Well, I'm glad to have you back, and I know everyone else will feel the same way."

I felt a tremendous weight had been lifted off of my shoulders, and I vowed I would never again go down a path in life unless it was approved by God through fervent prayer. I could *feel* when I was going against God's will, so I would seek that forever and ever, so help me.

I resumed volunteering at Teen Challenge once a week, on Monday nights, helping out with the new students. I enjoyed it, and apparently Leanne Goff took note of my zeal. It was my second Monday back, since the wrong turn to New Orleans, when the Women's Director called me into her office.

"Hey Leanne, what's up?" I asked.

"I just wanted to talk to you about something."

"Go right ahead."

"Okay. I know you've worked at the grocery store for a while, and you like it there. But what do you think about working for Teen Challenge?"

CHAPTER 90

February, 2001:

February in Michigan is a cold spot on the globe, especially to a native southern girl, but I had applied for and gotten a job at the Teen Challenge Sister's Maternity Center in Lansing.

Six months earlier, I had accepted Leanne's job offer and became a staff member for Teen Challenge Chattanooga, finally moving on from my cashier position at the grocery store. I prayed about it and felt positive vibes in my heart and mind, so I made the change.

After some further training, I actually became an instructor myself, and it was fulfilling to help new students in the program, as I had been by Soraya and Sandra. In some ways it didn't seem all that long ago since the carrot cutting incident, when I, as a newcomer to the program and relatively new Christian, had been lovingly rebuked for my attitude by the longsuffering Sandra Collier. But two years had passed and I was now a teacher, showing addicts the way to recovery and redemption in the way I had been shown.

I was free and single at that point, but I wasn't even thinking about a relationship or making a move without God's direction. I had not known real love in many, many years, and there was a time, especially in my years as an addict, when I had believed I would never again. That changed, though, when Soraya spoke about God having a future husband in the world for me. She, being single, was also trusting God to bring her a husband, and she inspired me to believe again that love was possible.

I made my list of the character and qualities I wanted my husband to have, and continued to pray about it each and every day.

I prayed that he would be empowered to be a strong husband, slow to anger, righteous and fair. I prayed that God would fill his mind with wisdom, and his heart with love and understanding. I prayed that he would never question my past, or throw it up to me, that he would trust me in all respects. I prayed that he might have gone through Teen Challenge himself, so that he would understand the discipleship programs. It would make it all so much easier! I prayed he would love animals, the way I did.

I essentially prayed for everything I wanted in a man, figuring if I got half of that, I would have a good one!

It was rewarding to work as an instructor at Teen Challenge Chattanooga, especially getting to know a woman named Robin, that ambitious, visionary soul with a dream to build a facility in Athens for The Women's Program she was facilitated with. She would visit our facility, follow the staff around, and ask us pertinent questions about the day to day operations, gleaning all the information she could.

"I feel God calling me to build in Athens," she told me one day after I gave my testimony to female inmates at a jail chapel service. That was part of my job during that time. I arranged speaking engagements and informed would be students about the Teen Challenge program.

"Well, you have to do it then, Robin," I replied.

"I will," she said resolutely, her jaw set, and I knew she meant it.

She was a whirlwind, setting up fundraisers, raking in the cash, and construction began in short order.

As involved as I was, I still felt the need to move on to another place, another town. The Urban Missions School in New Orleans had been a mistake, but staying put in Chattanooga was also. My life had dramatically changed, and I wanted a fresh start, a place where there weren't constant reminders of the things I had done and all I had lost.

I had confided to another one of my mentors my desire to relocate, and when I looked at the job posting she told me about on the Teen Challenge website, I was convinced it was where I belonged. I had a strong desire to work with babies, to learn to care for them, both to experience what I had missed with my two daughters as infants, and to prepare myself for, if God blessed me with it, another child someday with my future husband.

I prayed hard about it, and believed God's hand was working in my life.

When I got the call from Lansing, informing me the position was mine, my feeling was confirmed and I was elated! Here was my chance to start anew, and who knew what God had in store for me there? I was going on faith, trusting Him, and that's *never* a mistake.

There were plenty of tears as I said my good-byes to the staff in Chattanooga. I somehow knew I would never return, and it was bittersweet. I wished them all the best and God's blessings.

I parked my car at my mom's, and she was generous enough to give me the money for a flight to Lansing.

"Go and be good!" she told me, hugging my neck. "I'm so proud of you Shannon!"

On the flight, I looked out the window at the land below, and the clear blue sky above. *The page has turned*, I thought, *and I'm beginning a new chapter in my life. Please help me God, as I go forward."*

CHAPTER 91

Even though I'd had two babies of my own, I hadn't taken care of either one of them, so there was a learning curve when I arrived at the center. These were the babies of addicted mothers who gave birth in the program, and my job was to care for the infants until such time as the mother was capable.

I had never even changed a diaper before, but I learned to, among other things associated with post-natal care. I privately imagined they were my own at times, that I was taking care of Tiffany or Allison as infants; but I couldn't stay in that imaginary place long, lest feelings of regret and guilt overtook my mind.

I had my own apartment in Lansing, and the only time I went out, other than for work, was to engage in the events - rallies, lunches, concerts etc. - staged by Teen Challenge.

There was a men's center across town, and the female staff from the maternity center (numbering eight) would join with the fifty or so men. There were strict policies in place concerning fraternization; it was not allowed in any shape or form. At functions, the men had to stand or sit in front of the women so they would not be tempted to flirt with or ogle the females.

All of the staff and students at the center attended a huge church one Sunday, early in my employment, and there was an unusual moment, after the service, when a lady approached me.

"I have a word from the Lord for you, young lady," she said. "I don't know you, of course, but it was laid on my heart that the Lord is going to show your husband to you this year. You've been praying for him. He's not yet a pastor, but he's going to be. He'll be all you have prayed for. That's all I have."

I looked at her in wonder. "Who are you?"

"Doesn't matter, dear," she replied, smiling. "All that matters is that I told you what the Lord commanded."

"Well, thank you," I said, and she walked off, message delivered, message received.

There is a hierarchy at Teen Challenge, as with any organization, beginning with the Executive Director and his wife at the top and going down to one's immediate supervisor. There was never cause for interaction or communication between a staff member and the Executive Director, which is why I was bewildered when I was summoned one day, four months into my employment, to his office.

"Come in, Shannon," Jeff greeted, and then turned to the pretty woman by his side. "Shannon, this is my wife Shannon!"

We all laughed. "Good to meet you," she greeted me.

He went behind his desk and waved me toward a chair, while his wife sat off to the side. "Have a seat."

I did, and folded my hands in my lap. *What is this about*? I wondered. My mind was racing back over my time here, various things I had done in the course of my duties. I hadn't set the place on fire or accidentally killed a baby or anything, so what was goi...

"Shannon, we just need to address something with you," Jeff said, smiling, and I was thankful he started speaking to stop my rambling thoughts.

"Yes?" I replied.

"Has any male contacted you within the program? Flirted with you or tried to get your attention?"

"Absolutely not!" I barked a bit too loudly, and then took a deep, calming breath. "No, nothing like that has happened. I don't want to have a relationship unless it's ordained by God, to be honest. I'm perfectly fine with being single the rest of my life, if the only choice I have is mine alone."

Jeff and Shannon stared at me, and then Jeff leaned forward on his elbows and looked at me intently.

"Shannon, a staff member from the men's facility has approached us concerning you," he said. "He says he saw you from a distance at one of the rallies, and God spoke to him in that moment, putting it in his heart that you would be his wife."

I simply stared back at them, unsure of what to say to that.

"I don't know what to say to that."

"So you haven't *felt* anything, no message in your heart?"

"Nothing," I affirmed.

"Well, we want you to pray about this Shannon, see if there's anything you're not noticing. You've been a Christian for a while now, and God has performed a lot of miracles in your life."

"Amen to that."

"So you'll pray about it? Seek His guidance in this matter?"

"I will."

"Good!" Jeff said, standing, and that meant the meeting was over. "We'll call you back in here at a later date and see if anything has changed. I won't set a date; don't want you to be anxious about it, okay?"

"Okay. Thank you."

I walked out of the office, as perplexed as when I arrived. Some man says God talked to him about me? That I was going to be his wife?

I was open to all avenues, as long as it was God's will.

CHAPTER 92

"So you're all going to be required to give an eleven-minute sermon at the drop of a hat," the supervisor informed us in a staff meeting, the first one after Jeff and Shannon had dropped that bomb on me. I had been fasting some since (I didn't like it; who does? Giving up something you enjoy? But I wanted to hear from God about my future husband, if he was among us, so I did it) and praying, trying to feel something, opening my mind and heart.

The meetings were comprised of all male and female staff members from the men's center and the maternity center, and I found myself glancing furtively at the males, without expectations or prejudice. I wasn't looking for the cutest one. I had no regard at all for what he may look like. I just thought if he saw me looking his way, he might wink at me or something. But there were no indications whatever from any of them, and I felt no stirrings in my heart.

"We'll give you three weeks to prepare, and you may be wondering: why only eleven minutes?" the supervisor continued. "Well, your audience are addicts, like you were, and their attention span is short, about ten minutes, before they wander off. You have to get your message done in that amount of time so it will stick. Got it?"

We all affirmed we had gotten it, and the meeting was soon adjourned.

I went about my job and daily duties at the center: teaching classes, counseling students, leading devotions and singing during worship services, staying busy and trying not to let the wonderings and thoughts about who the mystery man was occupy too much space in my head.

It was exciting, however, to contemplate that I could be happy and in love again all these years later, that the normal life I had dreamed of and sought after in the past may finally come true for me. I had turned to drugs to escape a less than ideal childhood, a little girl who was denied the foundational experience of her father, and further, was traumatized by him. As a result I sought attention from anyone who would offer it, affirmation that I was *someone* in this world worth spending time with. I did not find it, running away from my past and running toward something I did not know, that I could not see, seeking love and confirmation that it was okay to just be me.

And then one day I found all the love, strength and confirmation I would ever need in my Savior, and it was more than okay just to be me.

It was all *right*.

CHAPTER 93

We began giving our eleven-minute sermons (the females went first), and I was fortunate to get mine out of the way early on. The audience (the supervisor and fellow staff members) would critique the speaker at the end, writing anonymously on a sheet of paper, pointing out mistakes or providing suggestions.

The sermons were preceded by a song service, and I was regularly part of the choral group on stage, singing like a bird. I always tried my best to make a joyful noise, and when the singing was done we took our seats on the stage, behind the podium. The supervisor then called the next speaker.

"Scott Reynolds, would you please come up and present your sermon?"

I didn't pay that much attention as he walked down the aisle. I was preparing to listen to what he had to say and take notes, but I did notice he was tall. I was seated behind him, so I couldn't see his face, which was good in a way - the listener wasn't distracted by a visual and nothing but the pure message could come through.

His sermon was on the Good Samaritan, and I was riveted by his words and the sound of his voice, his delivery, so easy and smooth. The minutes went by, and I suddenly felt a light, almost effervescent feeling flood my soul. I was covered in chill bumps as a divine truth was laid upon my heart, a message as clear as church bells:

This is your husband.

An unequivocal statement of fact, and I almost gasped aloud, but caught myself, covering my mouth. I stared at him as he wrapped up his sermon. This super tall guy was my future husband? He didn't look like the type I was normally attracted to, but I was certain about what I felt.

I didn't make myself known to Scott that day, nor did he approach me or give any indication of his feelings. In the weeks after, I kept my emotions within the confines of my heart, choosing not to share with anyone what had been revealed to me.

The time to share came, of course, when Jeff and Shannon called me back into their office. It had been two months since they told me I had a secret admirer, and I took a seat across from them.

"So, Shannon, did you pray about it?" Jeff asked.

"I did," I replied.

"And did God speak to you?"

"I think so, I think He has. Is it... Scott Reynolds?

"Jeff and Shannon looked at each other with mouths agape and eyes wide, and I heard Shannon take in a sharp breath. Then they looked at me, shaking their heads in wonder.

"Yes, it is," Jeff confirmed.

CHAPTER 94

Jeff and Shannon continued staring at me, saying nothing, and I broke the silence.

"So what happens now?"

Jeff rubbed his hands briskly together and smiled. "Right, well, we're going to introduce you to each other."

"This type of thing rarely happens, Shannon," Shannon said. "But it's clear that God is working in this to bring you two together."

"But when God brings a couple together, the way He has with you and Scott, we have to be really careful to make sure you two are setting a Christian example to the student body," Jeff stated.

"We will introduce you and Scott to each other, but it's not going to happen quickly," Shannon said. "We'll contact you when it's time, okay?"

"Okay," I agreed. What else could I do?

I went back to my apartment and hit my knees, thanking and praising God for continuing to work miracles in my life. I was excited about meeting Scott; but fearful too. I wanted to be a good companion for him, and I wondered if he knew anything about my sordid past as a prostitute and drug addict.

I knew that conversation would have to take place at some point, and it was an uncomfortable thought. But the Lord had brought me this far, and I trusted Him to help me with everything I encountered. I was grateful that I would not have to be alone much longer, and excited about the prospect of love again after so many years.

CHAPTER 95

March 20, 2001:

The day finally arrived when Scott and I would meet, and it was to be at the residence of the Director and his wife, an intimidating fact in itself (as if I wasn't nervous enough about meeting Scott), but Jeff and Shannon were wonderful hosts and they made me feel right at home from the start.

Meeting Scott was awkward initially, but he displayed a wonderful sense of humor over dinner, breaking the ice and making me laugh more than I had in a long time. I could check that one off the list of qualities I was looking for!

Before the night was over I felt I had known Scott all of my life, and I was certain he was the one God meant for me. Further traits I had desired became evident as the night wore on - he was a true gentleman, and exhibited a kind nature.

After dinner, Jeff and Shannon sat down with Scott and me to go over some ground rules in our relationship.

"I can't stress enough how important it is that you two are good examples, as a couple, to the student body," Jeff said. "The time will come when they will know about you, but not yet, okay?"

We simply nodded our heads in the affirmative and listened.

"You may talk on the phone for now, but only during lunch or after 10PM, when the students are in bed, and no more than thirty minutes per day. Now, we can check your phones (our cell phones - and back then it was the combo two-way radio/cell phone - were provided to us by Teen Challenge) and get a print out of times of calls and know if you're breaking, or abiding by, the rules."

As he was speaking, I thought about the fact that Scott was at least forty-three years old. I was thirty-one, and there we were, taking orders on our relationship like we were teenagers. It seemed silly in a way, but for addicts, rules, and obedience to them, are necessary, at least to a certain point.

To be clear, we could have abandoned the program, told Jeff and Shannon "We got this."

But we were dedicated to Teen Challenge and God's calling, and wouldn't dare do a thing to upset the future we believed God had planned for us.

CHAPTER 96

The next night, after 10PM, I was in my room, anxiously awaiting Scott's call. When my phone rang, I slid off the bed onto the floor, sitting cross legged and playing with my hair.

"Hey Shannon!" Scott greeted. "I didn't wake you, did I?"

"No! Are you kidding?" I replied, chuckling nervously.

"Well, actually I am. I was hoping you might be looking forward to talking. I had a great time with you last night."

"And I did too. With you, I mean."

"It's awesome, isn't it? How God spoke to each one of us about each other? It was like He sat down next to me and pointed you out!"

"Yeah, I felt the same way when you were preaching that night."

"Jeff and Shannon are great, right? You know, Jeff and I go way back."

"Really?"

"Yeah, we graduated together out of the Muskegon Teen Challenge Center, let's see...about twenty years ago. Hard to believe it's been that long! Pastor Phil McClaine ran that program, and he was a great man of God. I wouldn't be where I am today without him."

"That's great!" I responded, and although excited about being on the phone with my future husband, giddy with expectations of romance, I was also filled with trepidation for the question I knew would soon come. And in the next breath, he didn't disappoint.

"So how did you come into Teen Challenge?"

I could have skirted the question, answered vaguely, omitted some things about my past at this point, but I knew it was best to get it out of the way. It would all come out sooner or later.

So I took a deep breath and said:

"Well, Scott, I was a crack addict and a prostitute," I began, and went on to tell him my life's story. It wasn't a synopsis, nor was it in extreme detail, but he got the picture, and about the time I finished I heard a bell going off on his end.

"Time's up!" he said.

"You set a timer?"

"Sure! I wouldn't *ever* hang up with you if I didn't!"

"So, you'll call me back tomorrow night?" I asked anxiously. I had the thought in the back of my mind that upon hearing my story, Scott might bolt, exit stage left, say *"no thanks, babe, that's a bit too messed up for me."*

"Of course, I will! Listen, God has ordained us. There's *nothing* you or I have done or could do to stop that. Gotta go! Goodnight!"

He rang off, and I stared at the wall, tears forming in my eyes.

"Thank you, my precious Lord," I whispered. I felt a thousand pounds lighter with that full disclosure off my chest.

Now it was time for Scott to tell his story to me.

And it would be an amazing one, indeed.

CHAPTER 97

"I had a relative who was big time drug dealer in central Ohio," Scott started off telling me the next night. "He kept me in cocaine, and I never had to pay for it. Free drugs."

"Wow," I replied, imagining the kind of trouble I would have been in if drugs had been free to me. I probably wouldn't have been alive at that point.

"I started drinking when I was seventeen, and everybody knew about that. But the drugs, that was a secret between me and my relative. But even doing drugs, I was young enough back then to play some pretty good basketball. "

I knew about Scott's accomplishments as an athlete from his testimonies - at six feet seven inches tall, and big in stature, he was a standout basketball player at Galion High School, helping the 1974-75 teams to the most wins in school history and a league championship. Several schools made offers, and he chose to accept a scholarship from Cumberland College. But he hated studying, only wanting to play basketball, and may have continued with some success but for a car accident. He was the driver in a car full of teenagers, and in the crash, Scott suffered a head injury. He dropped out of school not long after.

"I was almost always stoned or buzzed, Shannon," he continued. "One of the saddest things was when me and some buddies were fishing on Lake Erie. The boat capsized, and one of the guys drowned. I was rescued, along with the rest, by the coast guard. It's a wonder we didn't drown too."

"I'm so thankful you survived," I said.

"Thanks. You'd think that would have sobered me up, right?"

I thought about my own weakness over the years, during the depths of my addictions.

"I understand," I replied softly.

"Anyway, I tried school again, you know about that."

He enrolled and played basketball, with former teammates from GHS, at Mount Vernon Nazarene College; but his alcohol and drug abuse increased, and he dropped out again, this time for good.

"I went into the Marines, and dedicated myself to it for the first three years, wanting to make a career out of it."

"Did you sober up?" I asked.

"Well, I slowed down some, but I was still hitting it, you know. It was before the military started drug testing. The big deal was the money I was making smuggling drugs out of Thailand, the Philippines and Japan!"

"What kind of drugs?"

"LSD. Had a supplier out of California. I got busted in Okinawa that was in...1983. Sentenced to five years in a Japanese prison! Boy, let me tell you, it's nothing like the prison system in the good ole U.S.A.!"

"I bet."

"Couple of bowls of rice and fish heads every day."

"Yuck."

"So the first thing I did when I got released was get drunk. Can you believe it?"

I most definitely *could* believe it. I had been there myself, where the demons are in control.

"Anyway, in 1990 I hit my lowest point, Shannon. I was ready to commit suicide. I don't know how I got there, but I wound up at my Aunt Alice's home, crying and miserable. She began telling me about God, that He loved me. I listened to her, having nowhere else to turn in life but to death, at that point. My sister, Sarabeth, came and got me and took me to the Teen Challenge center in Muskegon,

Michigan. I just went along, needing something other than the going nowhere but down life I was living."

"Amen!" I said.

"There's the timer!" Scott said. I was already hating that thing. "I'll continue this tomorrow night, okay? Got to stay inside the rules!"

"Okay," I said dejectedly. "Good night, Scott."

CHAPTER 98

Teen Challenge was founded in 1960 by David Wilkerson as a Christian faith-based organization intended to help teenagers, adults and families dealing with substance abuse. Mr. Wilkerson's first convert was Nicky Cruz, at the time the ruthless leader of a major New York City Puerto Rican gang named the Mau Mau's. His conversion was depicted in the 1970 movie *The Cross and the Switchblade,* with Erik Estrada playing the part of Nicky Cruz and Pat Boone the part of David Wilkerson.

After graduating La Puente Bible School in 1961, Nicky and his wife Gloria moved to New York City to help Dave Wilkerson with the development of Teen Challenge. Nicky became the first Executive Director at Teen Challenge for the Spanish Division. Over three years, Nicky and Dave worked together, praying and laboring to create the rehab and discipleship programs that have proved so successful to this day. But Nicky and Gloria felt the Lord's prompting to continue their evangelism, and left Teen Challenge to found the Nicky Cruz Outreach for Youth, a rehab and discipleship program for men, women and children. They ran this highly effective program for seventeen years, Nicky continuing his travels as an evangelist all the while.

Nicky Cruz has been extremely influential in the Kingdom of God, the author of seventeen books, including his successful autobiographies, *Run Baby Run* and *Soul Obsession,* and his latest book, *The Devil Has No Mother.* Currently, he is the active Executive Director of TRUCE, an urban evangelism training and outreach program, and he continues to travel the world, preaching the Gospel, a powerful voice for the Lord.

In 1990, Scott Reynolds entered the Teen Challenge program and accepted Christ, never looking back.

"I trusted Jesus, just like you, Shannon," he told me the next night. "I didn't think I could ever live with the sins

I committed, the things I had done, but I found out I didn't have to. Jesus saved me, forgave me, and took them away. It's amazing isn't it?"

"Yes it is, Scott," I replied, "And so are you."

There was a thick pause before he spoke.

"I'm going to say this, Shannon, because it's been true from the moment I saw you," he declared, drawing in a breath. "I love you."

"Oh, I love you too, Scott!" I exclaimed, and I began to cry, for the all the years I had wanted to feel love and be loved; for all the years I had longed to hear someone say it as sincerely as Scott just had; for the feeling of gratitude and thankfulness, in that moment, from my heart to God for bringing me to that place where hope resides, where all things are possible.

CHAPTER 99

The thirty minutes per day phone calls went on for about two months before Jeff and Shannon invited us back to their home.

"Thank you for sticking to the rules," Jeff said, addressing Scott and me after dinner, his wife Shannon by his side. "We checked the phone records and found you stayed within the limits. Now it's time for another phase."

"You can't sit together in chapel or the cafeteria yet," Shannon said, "it's not time for the students to know. But what we want you to do is contact other married staff couples, go on double dates and quiz them about their marriage. Ask them what their biggest problems are? Just pick their brains in general."

I left that to Scott, as he knew the staff better than I, and before long we went on our first double date with Pastor Tom Little and his wife Carolyn. They weren't staff members, but they came to preach occasionally at our services, and one of Pastor Little's sermons, titled *Pick Your Fruit*, has stuck with me over the years, the gist of it about being a fruitful Christian, not one that produces sour or rotten fruit, but sweet, vibrant fruit so others would see Christ like qualities in your actions and behavior.

I was glad they were the first couple we went out with. They were and are such wonderful people, and to begin with them was an easy start.

After a few dates with Tom and Carolyn, we branched out with other couples, and had a great time meeting them all.

I sought advice from any and all married women, especially those older than me, and one who was dear to my heart and helped me so much was Mama Sue. She was an awesome woman of God who dispensed valuable advice to me almost daily, and I can still hear her words of wisdom and comfort.

After three months of double dating and making new friends, Jeff and Shannon took us before the student body in the assembly hall one day, seating us behind them on the stage.

"I want to announce a couple to all of you," Jeff addressed the crowd. "Scott Reynolds and Shannon have been ordained by God and will be husband and wife one day. You will see them together from time to time, but please don't bug them, okay? Just go about your business as usual, but I wanted you all to be aware of them."

It was sort of awkward for Scott and me to be up there on display like that, but we hung in there, understanding these were necessary steps in our development. The day would soon come when we would stand before God and be married, and what a great day that would be.

CHAPTER 100

In total, there were nine months' worth of phases Scott and I had to go through, but the restrictions were lifted each time as we neared the end.

At seven months, Jeff and Shannon advised us to go outside of the Teen Challenge program to seek the required pre-marriage counseling.

"We are too close to you," Jeff said, and Shannon nodded in agreement, smiling. "We're your friends, and Tom and Carolyn feel the same way."

Pastor Ivan, of the local Assembly of God, was recommended, and he counseled us on things like unconditional love, financial matters, etc. He and his wife had been married fifty years, so he spoke from experience!

On the day of our wedding, as Pastor Tom Little conducted our ceremony, Scott and I stood before God and an audience of family and friends.

Standing there in my wedding gown, looking into my soon to be husband's kind eyes, I was a girl far removed from the drug addicted prostitute of yesteryear, one who lived in reckless abandon for the next hit. That old me was forever dead, and so were the voices that condemned me.

My biological father was not there to give me away. I had not spoken to him in years, but I was certain he was somewhere drunk or stoned, unaware of the world around him, his days burning up and away.

There was once a little girl who hid in a closet, clutching a doll to her chest, afraid of the man who beat her mother, a little girl who wondered what she had done wrong that her father wouldn't show her love.

But I did not need him anymore. I was no longer searching in vain for his affirmation in the touch or eyes of others.

God was my true Father and He was there on my wedding day, smiling down on me, approving and affirming me as I joined with Scott in Holy Matrimony.

My quest to find my father was over. I knew my heavenly Father loved me, would never let me down or let go of my hand, and would be with me all the days of my life, into eternity.

EPILOGUE

After our wedding in 2001, Scott and I took an in depth twenty-two-week course in *Pace Setting Leadership*, offered by Dave Williams Ministries. The class was very instructive and instrumental in preparing both Scott and I for future challenges as we took on various leadership roles.

Following that, in 2005 we were invited into Faith Fellowship International by Bishop Tim Cummings, and enrolled in New Creations Bible College in Richmond, Indiana. Scott was mentored personally by Bishop Cummings, becoming an ordained minister, and I earned a degree in Human Development and Behavioral Science, and became a licensed minister. While attending, we also worked with students in the New Creations Boarding School for Troubled Teens, where Bishop Cummings was Director.

In 2006, Scott and I accepted positions as Executive Director and Women's Director, respectively, at a Teen Challenge Center in the Permian Basin in Midland, Texas. The facility contained fifteen beds for females and sixty for males, as well as thirteen staff houses.

The center was heavily in debt when we arrived, and Shelly Trammell was a great help settling us in and showing us the ropes there.

Scott and I, along with Shelly, worked hard to raise money and get the facility back in black, holding fund raisers and bake sales and everything else we could think of.

In the middle of all that, I received a phone call from Roger Helle, the Director of Teen Challenge Chattanooga, inviting me to speak at a gala event there and offering to fly me in. I happily agreed.

It was special to stand up there and give my testimony to that audience, and after, I was approached by Roger Helle and Quinby Collier. Roger had a long, cardboard tube tucked under his arm.

"Shannon, Quinby here had a great idea!" he said, tapping the tube in his hand. "This is a $15,000 blueprint we used to renovate our facility. Quinby thought you might find use for it in Texas, and I agreed!"

He handed it to me with a smile and I took it, hugging his and Quinby's neck.

"Thank you both so much!"

We took that blueprint back to Texas, went into a fundraising frenzy and in less than a year we had a sparkling, brand new facility! I am forever grateful to Roger Helle and Quinby Collier for that blueprint, and to all the people of Midland for their generosity and contributions.

A year later, in the fall of 2007, we were incredibly honored to have Nicky Cruz as the keynote speaker at a fundraiser we put on in Midland Texas. Scott had taken a chance, figuring it couldn't hurt to ask, and called Mr. Cruz's secretary, requesting his attendance at our event. She passed on the message, and we were thrilled when he called back and accepted! It was a great fundraiser for us, and everyone there was awestruck by Mr. Cruz's presence and testimony, the riveting story of his conversion as a result of Dave Wilkerson's impassioned sermonizing.

In the spring of 2008, we attended the first major conference and banquet to mark the fiftieth anniversary of Teen Challenge, held in Lubbock Texas.

President George W. Bush was a major supporter of the Teen Challenge program, and not only did the President record a video that was played to the audience, he also sent his Deputy Assistant to the President, and Director of U.S.A.

Freedom Corps, Henry Lozano, a Teen Challenge graduate as well, to speak at the event.

Henry Lozano advanced the *Call to Service* initiative introduced by President Bush in his 2002 State of the Union address. Only ten *President's Call to Service Awards* (also referred to as the *President's lifetime Achievement Award*) is presented each year, to those citizens whose volunteer work and service in communities and causes rises above four thousand hours.

Henry Lozano himself received the award in 2005 in recognition of a lifetime of service.

Scott and I helped set up the itinerary for the banquet/conference, so we were in communication with the White House on a few occasions before the event. During one of those calls, it had been a matter of curiosity when the White House requested our social security numbers. We chalked it up to security precautions, but on the night when Henry Lozano spoke, the reason became clear.

"And for achieving the highest level of Platinum, with over 40,000 documented hours of service to the greater good of our communities and nation, I do present the *Presidential Call to Service Award* to Mr. and Mrs. Scott and Shannon Reynolds," Mr. Lozano announced, and both Scott and I were momentarily shocked. The crowd applauded and we finally unglued ourselves from our seats, made our way to the stage and accepted the award presented to us by Henry Lozano. It was such a high honor, and we also received an official certificate, lapel pins and a congratulatory letter from President Bush.

The year would continue in whirlwind fashion as in July we were flown to New York for another fiftieth anniversary celebration held at the Times Square Church. Scott and I stayed at the swank Hilton in downtown New York City. The evening before the service, I stood at the window of my hotel, looking out at the night lights of the Big Apple, remembering my long past days as a prostitute and drug addict in that state. I thanked God silently, in my heart, for saving me from that life. Oh, how rich in spirit I was now! He had given me the husband I had asked for, with every quality I desired, and a fulfilled life.

The next day, Scott and I were so honored to join Dave Wilkerson, Nicky Cruz, and Steve Hill on stage at the Times Square Church to take the offering. God had worked so much in and through those people's lives to effect change in the world for His glory, and we were blessed to be numbered among, and stand beside, them.

2008:

In September of that year, my mother called to tell me that my grandfather, Woodrow Parker Sr. had passed away, and that he had requested I perform the eulogy at his funeral. I caught a flight back to my hometown, and before I spoke, my lifelong friend, Kristi Caves, sung a beautiful song with heartfelt emotion as she remembered my grandfather from our childhood. As she sang, I could see that little blonde haired, six-year-old girl waving at me from behind my grandfather's house the day we first moved into the subdivision. It seemed like ages ago. When she finished, I took the podium.

"When I was a little girl, my grandfather was a refuge for me, a kind, generous and caring man who made me feel wanted and loved," I said. "I've never known a greater example of the Christian heart and life as the one he lived. The choices I made early in life led me down many a wrong path, but I know my grandfather's prayers were always with me, and the reason I am standing here now. His words of encouragement and advice have always been in my heart and mind. And although I am sad today that I no longer have him here on earth to talk to, I am happy for him, because I know that great man of God is in Heaven now, praising Jesus with the angels."

Six years after my mom and dad divorced, he fell in love and married a woman named Laura. They went on to have two children together - my brother and sister, Will and Kayla. I didn't get to know them well at all, as I was did not want to spend time around my drunken, deadbeat father, entirely unchanged from his old ways. Like he treated my mother years before, he physically and emotionally assaulted Laura until she left. He went downhill after their divorce, dying all alone in a filthy apartment, without a dime to his name, one year after his father passed.

I saw Will and Kayla at his funeral, but lost contact with them in the years beyond. I began seeking them out one day, on social media, asking friends if they knew anything about them, and then I received a friend request from Kayla. She had been searching for me, as it turned out, and it was wonderful to hear that she was doing well, and had just had a baby. I also learned that Will graduated college and worked for a prominent attorney in Chattanooga, TN. We stay in contact, and I am very grateful to have them back in my life.

2012-2019:

Scott's Mother was dying, so we left the Teen Challenge center in Midland Texas, moving in with his dad in Ohio. We attended the church where his parents had been going for a few years, and when the pastor position came open, Scott accepted and was voted in.

In my Christian life, I have made a few mistakes here and there, had ups and downs, but today, none of my addictions or shortcomings cause me to prostitute myself or sell/pawn my nice stuff; nothing I do causes me to not show up for work or cheat on my husband. Each day I run to God with my issues, and believe me, all of us, as long as we are breathing, will have issues within ourselves and in our lives, there will always be something we will need work on. So, I welcome God's chastisement, because it's all learning and growing experience and I consider myself a willing participant in the forever school of God.

I am blessed and so thankful to have relationships today with my two grown daughters, my first, twenty-nine year old Tiffany, and twenty-two year-old Allison. Tiffany is a mother of two, and has had her own issues and struggles with drugs. But she is currently four years clean and sober. Allison has a beautiful baby girl and is pregnant with her second baby.

We communicate with them on a weekly/monthly basis. I would love more time and involvement in their lives, but I appreciate what I do have, because truth be told, I don't deserve any sort of relationship with them at all.

Not long after I left the Chattanooga Teen Challenge branch, Soraya Rivas, my counselor and role model as a newcomer to Teen Challenge, had her prayers answered when she met and married an awesome man of God named Joel. Together, they have two beautiful teenage girls and live in Ohio. Ironically, the town where they live is only thirty minutes from the small town in Ohio, where Scott and I live.

Shelly Trammell, my wonderful assistant at the Midland Texas facility, married Troy Clawson, Scott's Work Duty Coordinator there. Prior to their engagement, I shared my husband list with Shelly, as Soraya had with me, and she prayed hard over it until she received her answer. Scott mentored Troy, and when Scott and I resigned, Troy took over as Executive Director and Shelly took my position as Women's Director.

Shelly and Troy now reside in Abilene Texas, and we remain good friends to this day.

Annette, that tall, beautiful girl who befriended me and had my back on the streets, got clean ten years ago. She went on a magical, storybook journey after, meeting and marrying her "knight in shining armor", a successful Orthodontist. They are a beautiful couple, and now make their home in Tennessee.

Sandra Collier, the lady that demonstrated to me an efficient carrot cutting technique and set me on the right path early on in Teen Challenge when she straightened out my attitude, lives with her sweet husband Quinby in Iowa, where they regularly attend church.

Amazingly, two of the bullies in high school that tormented me are now Believers themselves and over the years since my salvation, have actually wrote me heart felt letters of apology for the way they treated me. That's an answered prayer, because I forgave them a long time ago.

Pastor Tom Little and his wife Carolyn, who married us, now live in Indianapolis, Indiana, and run a successful online counseling service.

Scott's sister Sarabeth, who was there to drive Scott to Teen Challenge that fateful day in his life, died in 1999.

Although Kristi Caves is still a Registered Nurse, who Scott had the pleasure of marrying her to her knight in shining armor, Herb Thomasson.   She worked as a teacher for one year, then returned to what she loves best - nursing. We remain best friends to this day.

My mom Yvonne Howard, still lives and works as a cosmologist, in the old hometown. I travel to see her as often as possible, and she is a beautiful woman to this day at 70 years old.

2020:

Today, we live in our own home, in a small town, close to Columbus Ohio. (YES WE ARE BUCKEYE FANS), less than a mile from my father in law, Jim Reynolds, who is eighty-nine years old and still going strong! Scott has been the pastor of the Howard Christian Church for almost 5 yrs. Recently, God has just moved him (us) in a different direction. We've really enjoyed being the leaders at HCC, as we have made a lot of lifetime friends along the way. We want all of you to know how much we have appreciated your love, prayers and support, especially while I have been in the process of writing this book. We sure will miss all of you!

In 2015 I went to school and became a cosmetologist, in the footsteps of my mother, with a full license to manage and do hair, pedicures and facials. I had always wanted to be what my mother was, professionally, having grown up in her salon. I knew so much of it already, so it was a natural fit for me. I also work as a front desk Receptionist/Booking Consultant at Comfort Inn/Choice Hotels.

Living the small town life, much like the town I grew up in, it is home for our family. Scott has an adult daughter from his prior marriage, Lauren Reynolds, and he and I have one child together, our seventeen-year-old son Chase Reynolds. He is a "chip of the ole block," tall and excelling in basketball, as his father did. He is a wonderful young man and we are so proud of his character development and scholastic achievements.

Twenty-one years ago, in a jail cell and at the end of my rope, I surrendered my life to God - my soul, my will, my heart and my mind. And although I have not been anywhere *near* perfect since, I pray daily for forgiveness and guidance. The Lord has blessed me abundantly, far beyond what I deserve, and I am forever thankful to Him for his grace and mercy.

ACKNOWLEDGEMENTS

First and foremost, I want to thank the Trinity (God the Father, the Son and Holy Spirit) for saving me and being with me every moment of every day of this life I have lived on earth, and for keeping me safe from harm's way. If you have read this book entirely, you will understand that I should have died many times over; but God had an assignment for me, a plan for my life, and He does for *you* too. No matter how worthless or unloved you may feel inside, please know that God loves you. All you have to do is sell out to Him, to seek Him first, and He'll guide your every step and bring peace to your heart and soul.

Throughout my Christian journey I have met so many wonderful people that have contributed to my discipleship and mentored me, and I want to recognize them here.

Firstly, thanks to my wonderful husband, Scott Reynolds, who has loved me unconditionally over our married life, and has put up with my quirks and idiosyncrasies - you have made me laugh *so* much. You are everything I ever prayed for. I love you dearly.

Thanks also to my precious father in law, Mr. Jim Reynolds. He is the hardest working, most energetic man I've ever met! He has shown me an abundance of love and kindness since the day I married his son.

Thanks and appreciation to our son, Chase, for putting up with all the moves, new schools, and the times Scott and I were busy with Teen Challenge. Being a staff member is not always an easy life, especially for the children, and there were times, I'm sure, he thought we loved our students more than him; but he never complained, and we are forever grateful for his understanding and support.

Special appreciation goes out to Soraya Rivas Canamar for the genuine interest, great advice, extreme kindness and encouragement she showed to me during my time at Teen Challenge Chattanooga.

Sandra Collier, you are the most amazing Christian lady I have ever met! I want to grow up and be just like you!

Thanks to Leanne Goff for introducing to me to one of the greatest gifts that God has available to us - WISDOM - and how important it is to seek it in every decision we make, whether large or small.

Steven Hill passed away in 2014, but I am still in awe and grateful for his obedience to God's voice in leading the Brownsville Revival for so many years. God used him to reach many souls, including mine, and he was a mighty influence in the progression of my Christian life.

Thank you to my precious momma, Yvonne Howard, who never gave up on me and prayed for me all those years. I love you, Mom!

I am thankful for my deceased step father, Gordon Howard, who, from the day he married my mother, assumed the role of my earthly father and treated me as his own. He was proof to me that great men exist. He loved my mother, and took Tiffany as his own, parenting her and raising her with amazing love and kindness. I'll see you in Heaven, Dad!

Would like to thank Gordon's precious daughters, my step sisters, for treating me just like family from day one, as well! I will forever have a place in my heart for all 3 of you!

I would like to thank Jan Morckel, for all her help in helping me edit this memoir, God brought (you) her, at just the right time!

And finally, I want to thank my magnificent ghostwriter, AARON KEITH HARTLINE, for his integrity, work ethic, attention to detail and bringing my story to life! We spent many hours in communication, and he tirelessly worked to make sure everything was correct in the telling of my story.

UPDATE: Since the completion of this book, on January 16, 2020, A.K. Hartline fought and lost his battle with ALS, and has gone to be with the Lord. I must say he never once complained and some of his last words to me were that he was his father's son, meaning with respect and adoration, that Walter, his dad, had raised him right.

I would like to say a special thank you to his precious beauty of a wife, Pamela, for tolerating all the late night texts and emails, as we, together, tirelessly worked on this book for two years, to get it right.

Any of you, who may have enjoyed this book, you can go on Youtube, and look up Keith Hartline, to hear all the wonderful music he produced in his lifetime, and if you look for A.K. Hartline in the book section of Amazon, you will also find numerous books that are fiction, but are pulled from his life experiences. You will not be disappointed. He was brilliant and brought to life, every song, every book and story that was ever published, I am just grateful that he offered to help me with mine… enjoy!

AFTERWORD

Although popular culture has sought to diminish the role of fathers in recent years, there is no doubt in my mind the negative impact on my life caused by the emotional absence of my earthly father. I believe a father's attention, love and example in the home, or lack thereof, has a tremendous effect on his children. The premise behind the title of my story, *Finding My Father*, is that God the heavenly Father is the most important relationship one can have, no matter how good or bad the relationship with one's earthly parents. If I would have been made more aware of Him, or tried early in my life to find Him, I know I would not have chosen the many wrong paths I took. My hope is that anyone reading this book will lay down the substances you are using to fill the emptiness inside and turn to your heavenly Father, who loves you and *will* fill that void forever in your heart, if you'll simply invite Him in.

When I finally did begin to seek God, it was Teen Challenge that took me in and helped guide me through my early Christian life. I cannot say enough about this wonderful organization! I have been through other rehab programs and nothing compares to Teen Challenge, a totally positive life-changing and life- shaping program. As stated earlier in this book, Teen Challenge was founded in 1958 by David Wilkerson as a Christian faith-based organization intended to help teenagers, adults and families dealing with substance abuse, and boasts one of the lowest recidivism rates of any program in the world with an 87% success rate among graduates. Don't lose hope, 90% of the Teen Challenges across the world are adult centers that carry the Teen Challenge name.

To apply for the program, adult or juvenile, go to Teenchallengeusa.com. On the site, find the "Center Locator" on the home page, type in your city and state, gender, and then click "find." The search will come back with the center that best matches your needs. There may be a waiting list (Teen Challenge is much in demand) and an entry fee, but don't lose hope - God knows your need, and He will help you. Pour your heart out to Him, and if you are genuine in your desire, He will make a way for you. If you have a family member or friend that attends church, get them to take you. Introduce yourself to the pastor and talk about Teen Challenge and your wish to get into the program - most pastors are familiar with Teen Challenge and its success rate; and if you are persistent, the church may eventually take up an offering for you, or sponsor you. Like most things in life, your success will be equal to your effort. How much energy did you put into attaining drugs? There were times I would have walked barefooted through knee deep snow for miles to get a fix! I'm sure that has been true for you too, so if you really want to get into Teen Challenge, pray fervently, partner with God and work hard at it.

If your lifestyle does not permit you to enter the Teen Challenge program, you can still conquer the demons and drugs that plague you and become a new person in Christ. First, if you have not done so, confess your sins to God. Repent of them and ask Jesus to come into your heart. It's that simple. Grace is a free gift from God, but know that becoming a Christian does not mean you will be perfect, or that life will be easy. After you become a Christian, find a church, study the Bible and talk to God, all day *every* day. But know this - God is a gentleman; He is not going to force you to serve Him. If you met a person you were interested in, you would get to know them by communicating with them, right? Same goes in your new relationship with Christ. Over time, if you talk to and interact with Him all you can, you will develop an awareness of God's will and direction, and He will help you in every aspect of your daily life.

If you are an addict reading this book, you know you didn't reach your bottom overnight. It took maybe three to five years, a steady decline before you reached that place where there was nowhere to go but up. Conversely, it will take time to build a solid relationship with God. Make no mistake, however; your salvation is *immediate*. No matter what you've done in this world, the redeeming blood of Christ will save your soul. *No one* is beyond the Grace of God.

As you progress in your walk with Christ, however, Satan will also be there, as he has always been. **Psalms 139:13 (NIV Version)** says -

For you created my inmost being; you knit me together in my mother's womb.

God has always known *you,* He *made* you, and Satan has been there from the beginning of your existence also, pursuing your soul. Even after you become a Christian, and your soul is eternally secure, he is still attempting to diminish or entirely stop your witness to the world for Christ. The Bible says he walks about as a roaring lion, seeking whom he may devour, and it is the truth! Satan is the condemning, lying voice in your head that spoke to you when you did drugs, telling you they were the way to happiness, and he won't stop trying to persuade you to go back. How do you fight him? How do you resist temptation? Each day, just as you get dressed in whatever clothes you decide to wear, put on your spiritual clothes as well. What is that? The Full Armor of God. Here's the Scripture: **Ephesians 6:10-18 (NLT Version):**

*A final word: **Be strong in the Lord and in his mighty power.** [11]**Put on all of God's armor so that you will be able to stand firm against all strategies of the devil.** [12]**For we are not fighting against flesh-and-blood enemies, but against evil rulers and authorities of the unseen world, against mighty powers in this dark world, and against evil spirits in the heavenly places.***

*[13]**Therefore, put on every piece of God's armor so you will be able to resist the enemy in the time of evil. Then after the battle you will still be standing firm.** [14]**Stand your ground, putting on the belt of truth and the body armor of God's righteousness.** [15]**For shoes, put on the peace that comes from the Good News so that you will be fully prepared.** [16]**In addition to all of these, hold up the shield of faith to stop the fiery arrows of the devil.** [17]**Put on salvation as your helmet, and take the sword of the Spirit, which is the word of God.***

*[18]**Pray in the Spirit at all times and on every occasion. Stay alert and be persistent in your prayers for all believers everywhere.***

So there it is. Suit up your spirit, pray and talk to God, and when Satan attacks, trying to introduce negative thoughts or bad memories into your mind, say, "I rebuke you Satan, flee from me in the name of Jesus!" and he will go, pronto! If you can't shout it, whisper it - that old devil will hear it just the same.

Wherever you are in your life, I hope this book has been a help to you. It was not easy going back and recounting my past, but if my story means the difference in just one decision for Christ, it was worth it.

And if you are incarcerated right now, I'm sure there is a Gideon Bible available to you. Please find it and read it. Inside you will find simple instructions on how to become a Christian, and helpful verses as you begin your wonderful journey through life with Christ.

You may feel unloved or unwanted, but rest assured, your heavenly Father loves you; you and I are His children, and He longs to be with us *every* moment of *every* day of our lives.

Now go find your Father!

The day we married Sept 16th 2001

Scott and I in 2003 in the beginning first couple years of marriage

Scott at his Pulpit in 2017

My Brother and Sister and I, in 2016

My childhood friend Kristi and I in 2008

Scott and I in 2012

Cosmetology school 2014

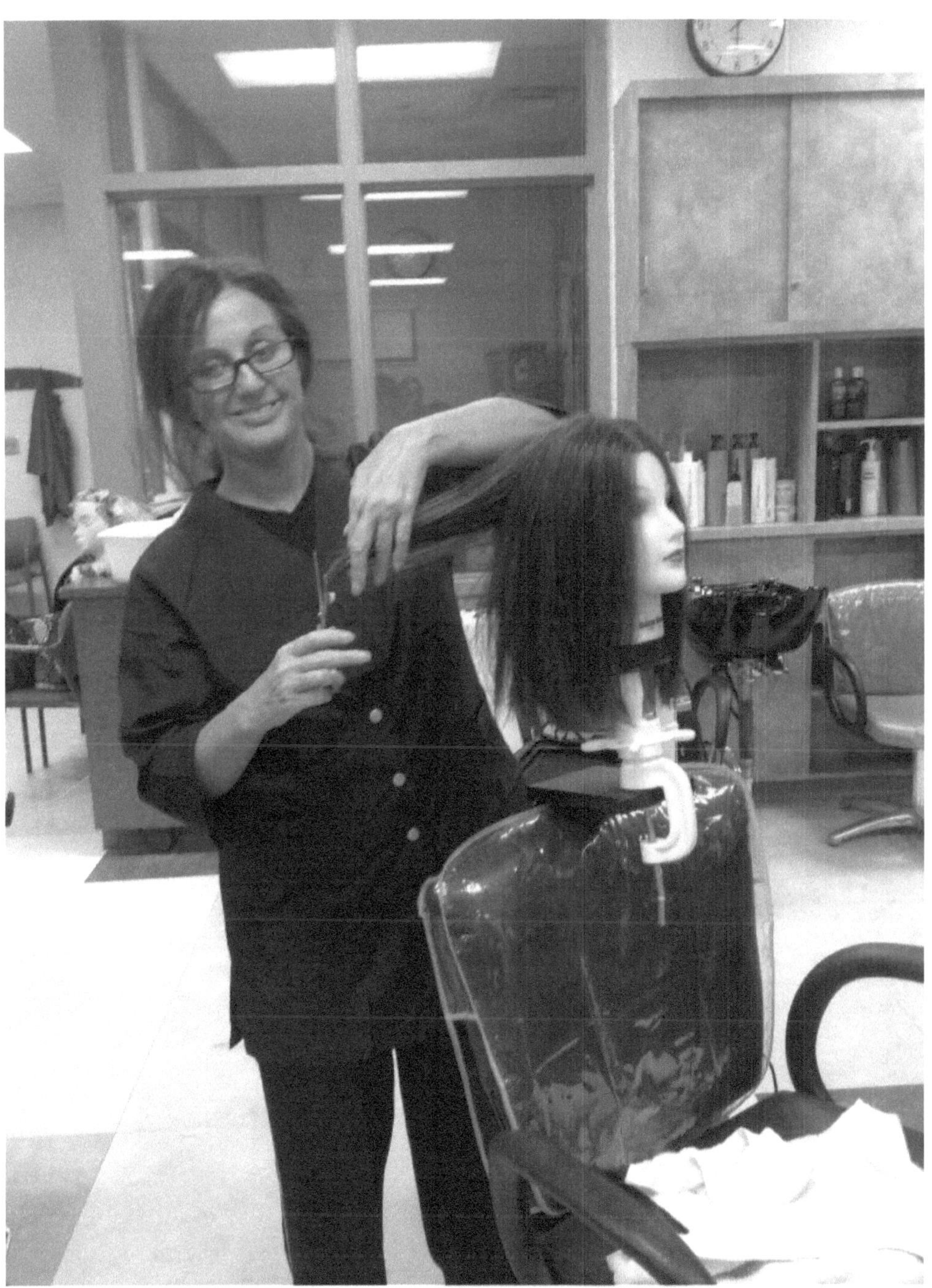

My "papa" and me, I loved him dearly

Our son Chase and our English bull dogs Bella and Brucey!

My mom and our son Chase

My second daughter and one of my grandkids

My son and second daughter

My awesome STEPFATHER GORDON HOWARD who died in 2000.

Shelly and me when I was the Women's Director of Teen Challenge of the Permian Basin and she was my assistant!

Edit
More
Edit

Scott, me and the famous Nicky Cruz

My friend Annette and I after we got saved and married to our Knights in Shining Armor, that we both prayed for!!

ONE LAST WORD! DON'T EVER GIVE UP! WE BOTH ARE LIVING BREATHING EXAMPLES OF WHAT GOD CAN DO WITH A WILLING PARTICIPANT! … AS LONG AS YOU ARE BREATHING, GOD HAS EVERY OPPORTUNITY TO GET YOUR ATTENTION AND SET YOU FREE…ITS NEVER TOO LATE… NEVER, EVER GIVE UP!!I LOVE YOU ALL!

THANK YOU FOR YOUR TIME.

Shannon Parker Reynolds